The Effective Supervisor's Handbook

The Effective Supervisor's Handbook

LOUIS V. IMUNDO

amacom

A Division of
American Management Associations

Library of Congress Cataloging in Publication Data

Imundo, Louis V.
  The effective supervisor's handbook.

  Includes index.
  1. Supervision of employees. 2. Personnel
management. I. Title.
HF5549.I48   658.3′02   79-54838
ISBN 0-8144-5571-9

Second Printing

This book is dedicated to my mother and father,
who taught me right from wrong
and the meaning of responsibility.

Preface

WRITING this book has been an enjoyable experience for me because for some time it has been something that I have wanted to do. The initial idea came to me a few years ago. For a number of years I had been conducting management development programs for supervisors as well as working with all levels of management to resolve or avoid employer-employee relationship problems. The more involved I became in training and in resolving employer-employee relationship problems, the more I found that supervisors played a critical role in those relations. It also became apparent that supervisors as a group were often the least trained members of management.

I have never been fully able to understand why higher levels of management do not take the time and invest the money to train and develop supervisors as managers. It has also been difficult for me to fully understand why higher-level managers often fail to consider supervisors' input in decision making. All too often I have found myself serving as an intermediary between supervisors, higher-level managers, and staff professionals. One message I have tried to leave with every client has been: Invest some time and money in training supervisors, require high performance, reward it when it is given, and listen to what supervisors have to say. If invested properly, the time and money spent will pay high dividends.

Over the years I have spent a lot of time reading about management, particularly about the supervision of people. I have found most books about supervision to be little more than so-called principles of management texts. To me many of those books lacked insight into the needs and concerns of supervisors. For the most part, they contained a lot of theory and little guidance for application.

I have written this book so it can be used by supervisors in any type of organization with all levels of employees. It can be used by supervisors who supervise attorneys, physicians, scientists, engineers, educators, electricians, carpenters, machinists, office personnel, and factory employees. Because the book has been written for supervisors in any type of private or public organization, the use of the word *company* has been carefully avoided. In its place the word organization has been used. Another word that has been carefully avoided is *subordinate*. To me *subordinate* communicates an image of an indentured servant. In its place the word *employee* has been used. Employees are not indentured servants; they are people who voluntarily join organizations and contribute their skills and energy in return for certain rewards and benefits from the organization.

I have been privileged to have worked directly with many thousands of supervisors in varied types of organizations. Much of what I have written in this book integrates their comments, suggestions, feelings, and criticisms. I have also tried to integrate my formal education and experience as a manager, educator, lecturer, and consultant. I have tried not to fill the book with too many of my own observations and experiences, but I have used those observations and experiences where I thought they would enhance, or contribute to what I was trying to communicate.

Supervisors are an important link in the managerial chain, and any chain is only as strong as its weakest link. Higher-level managers are, for the most part, well trained. How well they apply their training varies widely. Supervisors who are first-level managers are for the most part undertrained. In today's complex society, with its many challenges and opportunities, highly skilled managers at all levels, and the supervisory level in particular, are essential. I hope this book will make some contribution to the development of supervisors as managers.

In writing this book I attempted to use the terms *he/she, his/her,* and the like to show equal consideration to both men and women, but it proved to be awkward. Pronouns such as *he* and *him* have been used for literary convenience and are meant to apply equally to both men and women.

As usual, the author's debts exceed the numbers that can be reasonably acknowledged in a prefatory note. I am indebted to the many supervisors with whom I have had the privilege of working over the years. I owe a large debt to Harlan H. Todd and Vanoy (Bud) Faris, who a number of years ago gave me an opportunity to prove myself and influenced my thinking about management. Mrs. Joy Williams did an excellent job in meeting what often seemed to be impossible demands and time schedules. As is customary, any shortcomings in this book are solely my responsibility.

Louis V. Imundo

Contents

1

The management process
and the unique role
of the supervisor

OVER the past 30 years, a voluminous amount of literature has
been written about the process of managing. Much of this,
particularly the literature published in the past ten years, has
been misleading, redundant, and confusing. Unfortunately,
many of the people who write about management have never
successfully practiced it. Many writers, using their own style,
symbolism, and language, have interpreted, reinterpreted, and
often misinterpreted what has been said and done by others. In
addition, some writers, particularly academicians, are guilty of
viewing the management process on a limited scale and scope
and drawing sweeping general conclusions.

This is not to imply that everything written about management to date is inaccurate, incomplete, or impractical. On the
contrary, there are many excellent works. Unfortunately, it is
difficult for the average person to tell a knowledgeable publication from a poor one. Perhaps the most inaccurate position,
popularly held for some time, is that management is a recent
phenomenon. How some people could adhere to this belief is

almost incomprehensible. Even a cursory examination of the writings of philosophers, political advisers, economists, noblemen, military leaders, playwrights, poets, and historians makes clear that management has been applied to human endeavors and relationships since the beginning of recorded history. The Bible and the Koran contain numerous discussions about the process of management as applied to various facets of life. Many of the philosophies, processes, principles, and practices of management that were put in writing hundreds, even thousands, of years ago are applicable to modern life.

It can be argued that management touches every aspect of our lives. The success or failure of any society, any organization, or for that matter any one person can be directly tied to the effective or ineffective application of management. Problems are often caused by mismanagement and are corrected or avoided by effective management. Throughout our lives, we see and experience the effects of good and bad management.

Management does not apply only to business organizations. It is a universal process applicable to every aspect of our lives. To believe otherwise is to exhibit naiveté and myopia about human behavior. The methods and approaches used in managing business organizations can be applied, often with little or no modification, to managing relationships with spouses, children, friends, relatives, acquaintances, and strangers. We even apply management to maintaining our physical and mental health. It is the universality of the applicability of management that makes its study and understanding so rich and rewarding. Development of a management philosophy that can be successfully applied will pay dividends throughout our lives.

Management is the key activity that separates successful organizations from those that fail. To apply management successfully to different organizations and situations, it is important to recognize that each environment or situation is unique. If that uniqueness is not taken into consideration, the application of management that has worked in one environment or situation may not work in another. Many writers and practitioners of management have failed to recognize this and have erroneously concluded that management has only limited applicability.

Learning to apply management successfully is somewhat like learning to become a great chef. Assuming that most chefs receive about the same quantity and quality of training, will they all reach the same level of proficiency? The answer is no. What separates a successful chef from an average chef? What is it that separates a successful manager from an average manager? Is it drive? Ambition? Luck? It may be all of those, but it is mostly a matter of understanding how to apply their skills under varying conditions and situations. This requires knowledge, perceptiveness, and a sense of timing. Without this ability to sense the need for change and knowing how and when to implement change, failures will occur.

Another popular view is that supervisors are different from people called managers. It is interesting to observe that the current literature attempts to segregate managers by organizational level by using titles such as executive, manager, administrator, foreman, and supervisor. The attempts to segregate managerial levels and roles have led to considerable misunderstanding about the managerial process itself.

People in managerial roles, no matter what their titles, are managers, and they engage in the same basic activities. Managers who directly supervise people are generally regarded as supervisors. They are the first rung on the managerial ladder. Supervision of people is a vital part of the managerial process. Supervisors are managers. However, at higher levels in the organization, we often see the use of the title manager. What is the difference, if any, between a manager and a supervisor?

The difference, at times, is in the depth of activities. Whereas supervisors' activities primarily center around people, the activities of people titled managers are broader in that they deal not only with people, but also with markets, time, events, technology, machines, and systems that are both internal and external to the organization. Managers engage in such activities as supervision, administration, salesmanship, planning, training, development, and control. Supervisors, depending upon their organizational roles, may engage in many or all of the same activities. However, their primary responsibility is getting people to cooperate to meet explicit organizational goals. Because of changing values and attitudes, coupled with large, complex work environments, getting people to cooperate to achieve organizational goals requires an intensive effort coupled with a considerable degree of training and development.

Supervisory jobs vary extensively in scope, content, and application. In addition to being called supervisors, employees who directly manage the activities of nonsupervisory personnel may be titled: foreman, crew chief, unit director, superintendent, head engineer, head nurse, office head, or overseer. Supervisors come in all sizes and shapes; social, psychological, and economic backgrounds; religions; sex, ethnic origins, and educational backgrounds. The word supervision comes from the words *super*—meaning over and above—and *vision*—the act of seeing objects, or perceiving mental images, or looking over.

Supervising people is with little doubt the most complex and difficult aspect of managing. Today, as probably never before, the supervision of people at all organizational levels is facing intensive challenges and is receiving greater attention and emphasis. Supervisors, whether of factory, office, technical, or professional workers, are the direct link between the managerial structure and the operative structure of any organization. To employees, supervisors often represent the "organization." Workers' feelings about the organization, members of management, their jobs, and interpersonal relations are, to varying degrees, all affected by the relationship they have with immediate supervisors.

When, from a management viewpoint, employees develop less than desirable attitudes toward others, it is eventually apt to have some adverse effect on cooperation and productivity. Supervisors are therefore in a unique position, because their ability to discharge responsibilities properly has a direct and visible impact upon organizational productivity and profitability.

Many people in technical, staff, and even higher managerial positions fail to recognize or appreciate the tremendous demands that are put on people who directly supervise employees. Medical research has shown that supervisory positions can be very stressful and contribute to debilitating diseases such as heart attacks, ulcers, and mental depression. But research has also shown that human beings need stress. Stress can stimulate both physiologically and psychologically. The statement that some people work better under stress is true, and channeling stress into constructive results can be extremely satisfying. Stress debilitates people when they are unable to successfully manage it. To be able to successfully manage people requires considerable training and skill development. To place people in supervisory positions without the benefit of training is to invite the problems associated with the inability to manage stress.

The solving of technical and methodological problems can be assigned to nonsupervising specialists. The management of people cannot be assigned to those specialists. It must be assigned to supervisors who must act as generalists and specialists simultaneously. Supervisors must deal with employees who may be careless, lazy, hostile, hot-tempered, moody, or aggressive. Supervisors must be both production and human behavior engineers.

In the past, the role of the supervisor was far less complex and demanding than that of the modern-day supervisor. Supervisors of the past, like their modern counterparts, had to maintain cooperation and production, but they had far more authority. The controls and penalties imposed on employees for not complying with supervisors' directives were considerably more severe when compared with today's standards. Supervisors could force their authority over employees. Today, supervisors may still obtain cooperation by resorting to indirect force, but because of many complex factors they are more often called upon to use different approaches to managing. Today's supervisor is often frustrated by policies, rules, and regulations imposed by higher-level managers, staff specialists, collective bargaining agreements, unions, government restraints, and employee attitudes that are difficult to understand and accept.

Today's supervisor theoretically has the power to hire, transfer, suspend, lay off, recall, promote, reward, discipline, and adjust employees' grievances, or effectively recommend such actions. However, it is not unusual for decisions made by supervisors to be overruled at higher levels of management or by staff specialists. Even methods of organizing and directing work may be reviewed and overridden by staff specialists, higher management, unions, and laws. In spite of these limitations on authority, supervisors are expected to get the job done, and are held directly accountable for employees' performance. It is the supervisor, not the staff specialist or others, who must answer the questions when goals are not met and employees are not cooperating. Many supervisors long for the days when they had almost unilateral control over employees. The changes that have taken place in the supervisory role have not been without adverse effects upon supervisors. Many of them often feel confused, insecure, depressed, alienated, apathetic, and even hostile toward their work, workers, and organization. It is not surprising that these conditions eventually cause many problems for organizations.

Because supervisors are the link between workers and higher levels of management, staff, and technical specialists, they are often called upon to represent both employees' interests and those of higher management and staff specialists. If supervisors were to act only as management's representatives to employees, they would lose their effectiveness in getting employees' cooperation and meeting organizational objectives. If supervisors were to act only as employees' representatives, they would find themselves at odds with their supervisors and the organization. Successful supervisors must continually operate in a manner that permits organizational objectives and individual needs to be met. That is not easily accomplished.

Supervisors may be chosen on the basis of seniority, proficiency, favoritism, demonstrated leadership, experience in other organizations, or educational background. It is not unusual, and often is desirable, to select capable individuals from the work force for supervisory positions. Making the transition from being one of the boys or girls to being a supervisor is difficult, however, and requires a lot of drive on the part of the individual, as well as social, psychological, and educational support from higher-level managers and staff specialists. Usually only those who have made the transition fully appreciate the degree of difficulty.

The skills required of an effective supervisor are different from those required of a proficient worker. Selecting the best worker to be a supervisor is a common and dangerous practice. Because of the allure of more money, prestige, or status, good workers often accept supervisory positions, but they find out that being a supervisor is quite different from being a worker. Because they lack the skills or don't enjoy supervisory activities, they perform marginally or poorly. Some quit, and some are discharged. Others stay in supervisory positions because they don't want to lose face by asking to be taken out of the job and give up the additional pay, status, or prestige. People should go into supervisory roles because they want the challenge and satisfaction of supervision. If being a supervisor does not provide psychological income, that is, job satisfaction, challenge, recognition, and creativity, no amount of money can adequately compensate for the stress and other problems associated with the job.

Functions of Supervision

People should be placed in supervisory positions primarily because they have skills and traits that enable them to effectively engage in the activities of management. The primary function of managers at any level is to create, or help to create, environments where people are willing to cooperate to achieve common goals. In working toward common goals, people satisfy their personal needs.

Much of the literature written about management covers indepth functions or activities of management, which are usually identified as planning, staffing, organizing, directing, and controlling. Discussion of these functions often fails to capture the essence of the management process. Supervisors, as creators of environments, exert influence over people through formal and informal means. Supervisors are, in effect, manipulators. Many people confuse manipulation with exploitation. When people are persuaded to do something they don't want to do and benefit from the activity, they don't feel that they have been manipulated, even though they have been. When people are persuaded to do something they don't want to do and do not benefit from the activity, they often feel manipulated. They have then been exploited. Normally, people tend to avoid situations, conditions, activities, and relationships from which they do not benefit. In order to be effective, supervisors must have the skill to influence people in a positive way for mutual benefit to employees and the organization.

Supervisors must have conceptual skills. The ability to conceptualize is implicit in many of the activities that supervisors engage in. Supervisors must be able to conceptualize the technical and human aspects of work. They must understand people, job requirements, and work environments. They must understand what motivates people and to what ends they are motivated.

Supervisors must have interpersonal skills. Knowing individual and organizational needs alone is not sufficient. They must not only know these things, they must know how to put them together. How they approach people, how approachable they are, how they interact with people in terms of communicating and listening are all extremely important. Supervisors must develop a sense of timing. It is not enough to know what to say and how to say something, it is also necessary to know when to say it. Supervisors must recognize that each human being is unique, and must develop a personal relationship and approach to handling interactions with each person that enhances rather than detracts from their desire to cooperate. They must know how to tell people when they have not performed to standards, as well as how to tell people when they have met or exceeded standards. Interpersonal skills require knowledge of human behavior, maturity, and sensitivity.

Supervisors must also be effective communicators. They are continually selling their ideas to superiors, peers, and employees. Persuasiveness and perseverance are important in selling ideas. Supervisors, like other levels of management, usually have more responsibility than authority. To accomplish goals over the long run, influencing people to do things voluntarily rather than ordering compliance is usually more effective.

An important and often overlooked requirement of supervisory positions is the training and development of employees. Change in organizations is often essential to ensure continued survival. To meet changing organizational requirements, and to give employees opportunities to satisfy professional growth needs, training and development activities are necessary.

Planning is an essential activity for supervisors. It determines future actions to be followed; it requires an ability to see into the future. In the planning process, supervisors often act as internal antennae for higher levels of management. Since they are closest to the operational environment, they are in the best position to communicate information upward to aid in decision making. Without this necessary input, the probability of incorrect decisions being made increases.

Supervisors must be able to exert control when occasions necessitate its use. Unfortunately, not all people do the right things all the time. People deviate from what is required or expected either out of ignorance or out of intent. Supervisors have the final responsibility for insuring that requirements are met and objectives achieved. Although employees can be held accountable for their actions, the final responsibility rests with the individual who is in the leadership or management position. This being the case, it is essential that supervisors be able to impose various restrictions or controls on others. In some cases minor adjustments to activities or relationships are required, while in others a major overhaul and the assumption of total control are necessary.

Supervisors should participate in the staffing process. Staffing may be divided into two components: bringing people into the organization, and assigning them to the various jobs that are available, or will be available. Unfortunately, in too many organizations, supervisors have little input or control on the recruitment and selection of personnel. The placement of personnel in various jobs varies widely among organizations' practices. In some organizations, supervisors have considerable authority in determining who gets what job and how movements among jobs take place. In others, supervisory authority in this area is sharply curtailed by staff specialists, higher management, or unions. In a unionized organization, the labor-management agreement often stipulates the procedure to be followed in the placement of personnel in jobs. Job selection, job transfer, bumping, and promotion are other activities normally covered in labor-management agreements.

Supervisors should have a degree of technical competence in the work they supervise. When supervisors are promoted from within a work group, they often have a high degree of technical skill; indeed, their technical proficiency may be so high that removal from the work group could adversely affect its overall performance. It is not a necessary requirement that the most highly skilled worker be the supervisor for many, if not most supervisory roles. What is necessary is that supervisors have working knowledge of the type of work they supervise. When supervisors are selected on the basis of formal education, they may have developed skills at handling people, but they often do not have sufficient technical skills to function effectively. Significant problems occur in meeting organizational objectives when supervisors have limited knowledge of the work they supervise, and employees with the necessary knowledge refuse to fully cooperate. Generally, as supervisors are promoted to higher levels of management, the need for technical competence in the work supervised diminishes.

It can be said of many jobs that attitudes toward job responsibilities can and do affect the accomplishment of tasks. To be effective in the role of a supervisor, one must think and act like a supervisor. Acceptance of a supervisory position separates a person from other employees. As has been discussed, the job requirements are different from those of a worker. Supervisors are the formal leaders of work groups, and therefore the examples they set and the attitudes they exhibit affect the behavior of others. Good or bad feelings about work, peers, superiors, and employees in the organization strongly influence the attitudes of other people. Good or bad attitudes do not evolve in an instant; they develop over time.

A person does not normally wake up in the morning and say that he's going to have a good attitude about things and have that attitude persist. When people who are in supervisory positions do not understand the requirements and responsibilities of the role, or do not have sufficient training to discharge those responsibilities properly, they usually work under very frustrating conditions and circumstances. Frustration and other negative psychological feelings that persist over time are apt to cause poor attitudes. Supervisors who develop such attitudes will find that they are similar to an infectious disease. Supervisors must recognize the uniqueness of their role and the effect their attitudes and feelings have on others. Higher management and staff specialists also must recognize the uniqueness of the supervisory role, and in doing so, must consider three important points:

1. Supervisors are part of the management team and they should be treated as such. They must be accorded the full rights, privileges, and status of managers. Supervisors are expected to carry out the decisions made by higher management. When supervisors disagree with higher-level decisions, they must be allowed the opportunity to express their feelings.

2. Higher-level management and staff must recognize that on occasion their decisions have to be changed, in part or entirely, to meet the needs of employees and supervisors. Supervisors, as members of the management team, are in the best position to sense the pulse and temperature of the work force. In their role they are in the best position to provide input to higher management and staff concerning employees' feelings, attitudes, and possible reactions to, or from, higher-level decisions. If higher management and staff do not take supervisors' opinions and advice into consideration in decision making, they may find themselves in the position of having to force decisions on the organization at considerable social and psychological as well as economic expense. The net effect is that deteriorating cooperation starts at lower levels and progresses through the organization.

3. Staff specialists, in particular, must recognize the challenges and demands that are placed upon supervisors. They must provide for on- and off-the-job training and counseling as part of supervisors' development. It is unfortunate that many staff specialists, as well as higher-level managers, have not served in supervisory roles, especially at lower levels in the organization. Because of this lack of experience, it is difficult for many staff specialists and higher-level managers to develop

an appreciation of the demands that are placed upon people in supervisory roles. Meetings, group problem solving, personal job assignments, coaching, counseling, and training programs are not only desirable but a necessity. Supervisors need coaching, counseling, and training as well as understanding from higher levels of management and staff specialists if they are to develop and maintain the favorable work relationships and attitudes that can reduce organizational costs and enhance productivity.

Proper Supervisory Attitudes

Following is a checklist of attributes that exemplify proper supervisory attitudes. The reader's personal feelings and beliefs should be compared to each of the listed statements to determine if an attitude is proper, and if not, to help identify what attitudes need to be changed. Supervisors have the proper attitude if they agree with and practice the following:

• The primary responsibility of a supervisor is to create, or facilitate in creating, a climate where people are willing to cooperate to meet organizational objectives, and in doing so, serve personal needs.

• Supervisors should decide controversial issues on the bases of facts and circumstances. Matters involving employees should be decided on merit and not on personal sympathies to a particular employee or group.

• Supervisors must accept higher-level management and staff decisions and directives as sincere expressions of what should be done to meet organizational objectives.

• Personal feelings about organizational policies and higher-management and staff decisions are to remain private. They should not be discussed openly with employees, even though employees may be questioning a policy or decision that you do not personally agree with. Supervisors should discuss their disagreements privately with higher management or staff personnel. Supervisors have a legitimate right to ask for review of decisions that directly or indirectly affect themselves or employees.

- Supervisors must earn the respect, trust, and confidence of their employees.
- Supervisors must give credit to employees who do a good job. Recognition and praise, raises and promotions, should not be given on subjective bases, but on objective bases related to job responsibilities and the accomplishment of organizational objectives.
- Supervisors are responsible for the performance of their groups. They must therefore accept partial responsibility for the failures of employees. Employees may be held accountable for what they do and responsible for their segments of work. However, the final responsibility for output rests with the supervisor. Supervisors, in discussing the wrongdoings of employees with higher levels of management or staff persons, cannot say that it was the employees' fault and attempt to absolve themselves of any guilt whatsoever for employees' wrongdoings.
- Supervisors must be objective and fair in judging the actions of employees. Objectivity and fairness must be considered with a view to the value systems of supervisors, the organization, and employees.
- When employees require counseling or disciplinary action, supervisors must accept the responsibility and operate under the philosophy that corrective action has the objective of rehabilitating rather than punishing. Punishment may become part of rehabilitation therapy, but the basic objective of any corrective action is to rehabilitate the employee.
- Although it is not always possible or feasible, supervisors should attempt to allow employees to have as much authority or control over their work as possible. Organizational, technical, safety, legal, and human factors must be considered in determining how much latitude employees can be allowed without impeding production requirements. At the same time, delegation must stop short of abdication of control.
- We live in an era when all people are sensitive about their civil and industrial rights. Supervisors must see to it that employees' rights are respected. Implicit in this is that employees must be held responsible for their behavior. With every right, there is at least one concurrent responsibility.

- Supervisors are leaders, and leaders are responsible for setting proper examples for others to adopt and follow. Supervisors must manage with a high degree of moral integrity. They must communicate to employees the idea: Do as I do, which is the same as what I say.

- People have varying degrees of drive, intellect, and ambition to develop personally and professionally. Supervisors are responsible for facilitating employees' personal and professional growth on the job. Training and development activities are not just desirable, they are essential to meet human and organizational needs.

- Politics are an inevitable part of human interaction. Politics per se are not bad, but the results of political interaction and activities sometimes cause problems. Supervisors are responsible for channeling politics toward constructive, not destructive, results.

- Whenever people work together, conflict is inevitable. Conflict, like politics, is not bad per se. Again, supervisors are responsible for channeling conflict into beneficial rather than destructive results.

- Supervisors must be prepared to support employees in situations where employees are in the right. People respect other people who stand up for their convictions and beliefs. They also respect a supervisor who will take personal risk and stand up for them.

- As people of moral integrity, supervisors must be prepared to keep their word to employees. No leader can survive over the long run when his or her word cannot be trusted by others.

- Supervisors must maintain a work climate where employees can express their feelings and concerns openly, without fear of intimidation or reprisal.

2

Establishing and maintaining
effective working relationships

OVER the past one hundred years, a large body of knowledge about human behavior has been evolving and developing. Considering that knowledge, techniques for the application of theory into practice are at relatively low levels of development; and the majority of supervisors do not have sufficient training in the behavioral sciences to properly apply the techniques that have been developed.

Problems with employees may stem from one or many interrelated causes. Theoretically, it may be possible to identify the cause(s) underlying employees' unacceptable behavior. Identifying problems and their causes is one thing; correction is quite another. Solutions to problems are often elusive because most people, supervisors included, go about it the wrong way.

There are two ways to deal with problems. One is to treat the causes, and the other is to treat the symptoms. Treating symptoms is a hit or miss, trial and error approach, and is rarely as efficient or effective as dealing with causes. The symptomatic approach is used most often because it is easier and quicker. Treating causes is more difficult, especially since causes may be deeply rooted and complex. However, in the long run, this approach is often far more effective.

Needs and Behavior

Behavior is the result of people's attempts consciously or subconsciously to satisfy needs. Everyone has needs. Needs are the stimuli that trigger the motivation process. Motivation is the observed behavior that is directed toward satisfying needs. The needs of people can be identified and categorized. Considerable research has yielded sufficient evidence to show that people share a broad range of similar needs. However, the importance of a need to a person, the identification of needs that cause specific behavior, and how and why people organize and direct their behavior to satisfy needs are very difficult to understand. To be effective as managers, supervisors must develop a working understanding of motivational processes.

No two people are exactly alike. People share many similar traits and characteristics, and yet are very different. People vary physically, psychologically, and socially. Broadly speaking, all people have physical, psychological, and social needs. For some time it has been widely believed that people's needs exist in a specific order of importance, or what is called a hierarchy.

Within the framework of physical, psychological, and social needs, a broad set of subclassifications can be identified. Many of these subclassified needs embody more than one of the primary needs. For example, people need food to sustain themselves. Can we conclude that eating is a physical need? Do people eat to live, or do they live to eat? The act of eating, depending upon circumstances and conditions, may be far more social and psychological than it is physical. In the American culture, Thanksgiving with its traditional turkey and the trimmings is a ritual that is filled with symbolism. The preparation, eating, and post-eating phases are usually socially and psychologically as well as physically satisfying.

Following are some subclassifications of human needs. They are not categorized as physical, social, or psychological. Circumstances, conditions, perceptions, and values all interplay to make rigid classifications impossible. Countless writings by psychiatrists, psychologists, sociologists, and others have endlessly debated whether a need is social, psychological, or physical. People have needs for achievement, recognition, acceptance, power; self-respect, respect of others; justice, protection, opportunity; physical well-being, physical activity, relaxation; sexual gratification, love, companionship, friendship, compassion; freedom for self-expression, peace of mind.

This list could go on for many pages. It is evident that the identification of people's needs, which serve to stimulate behavior or the motivational process, is a difficult task. This does not imply that to manage people effectively supervisors must be psychiatrists or psychologists, but effective supervision does require a basic understanding of human behavior. Part of that understanding is common sense. Unfortunately, common sense is not all that common in people. If it were, there would be fewer problems with people in the workplace.

People's behavior is shaped by a variety of factors. First, human beings are not born with the same characteristics, traits, attributes, or abilities. To a degree, the traits, characteristics, and abilities inherited in the genes directly and indirectly influence behavior. No two human beings experience the same physical, social, psychological, and environmental conditions and influences throughout their lives. The physical, psychological, and social conditions of environments are forces that affect and effect behavior. People are in part products of heredity and in part products of environment and conditioning. When people work in an organization, they bring into that organization all their inherited traits, characteristics, and abilities, as well as their learned behaviors. Learned behaviors include anything that is formally or informally learned throughout a person's life. These traits, characteristics, and abilities in the forms of skills, values, personality, perceptions, beliefs, feelings, and attitudes are influenced by environmental and situational factors with resultant observed behavior. The higher the degree of similarity in people's heredity and environment, the higher the degree of similarity in observed behavior.

The Motivation Process

How many times have we heard someone say he is not moti-vated? Whenever we observe behavior, we are seeing the motivational process in action. Motivation is the action part of a need-satisfaction cycle. Whatever needs people have, con-sciously or subconsciously, at a given moment, will cause be-havior if some sort of action, activity, or reaction can be as-sociated with the perceived eventual satisfaction of the needs. For example, suppose someone whom you did not know calmly walked up to you and began to choke you. You might experience a variety of emotions such as fear, anxiety, rage, or anger; but because you are now in a state of danger, your primary need is to reach safety. You can clearly recognize your need and the seriousness of the situation. What do you do to get from danger to safety? Do you run, kick, punch, scream, submit, pray? The course of action you choose is based on your perception of what the best one is, given your subjective analysis of the different courses of action available and their probability of success under the present circumstances. You will engage in various forms of behavior, that is, your motiva-tional process, until you either die or achieve the goal of safety. If you engage in one form of behavior and it is unsuc-cessful, you may try another, and another, and even another. As people learn, either directly by experience or indirectly from the experience of others, they attempt to exhibit be-haviors and engage in activities that will best satisfy their needs as they see them at that time.

Much has been written about needs and whether or not they exist in any hierarchy of importance. Certainly not all needs have the same intensity or importance to people. Reflections on our own lives will show that something that was important to us at one point in life is unimportant at another point. For example, our spiritual needs generally tend to become more important as we approach death. When we are young, active, and healthy, our spiritual needs tend to be lower than in later years. This is a generalization, and for some the example does not apply. Research, observation, and logic do not support the idea of a common ranking of needs in a specific order of importance.

As the priority and magnitude of needs change, behavior changes. Needs interact with one another, but it is the strongest needs that tend most strongly to determine behavior. It must be remembered that when we discuss and attempt to analyze people's behavior, we are dealing with subjectivity and probability, which can be reduced when supervisors have a basic understanding of behavior and understand the people they supervise.

The basic principles of motivation are the following:

- Although needs can be broadly classified, their priority and intensity among people vary considerably; and they may vary according to situations and with time.
- In the vast majority of their daily actions and reactions, people are guided by habits established by motivational processes that are present at birth or arise during early stages of development and throughout life.
- Motivated behavior may be directed consciously or unconsciously toward the satisfaction of needs. It is basically a psychological process and as such it is not controlled by logic.
- Motivation, for the most part, is an individual matter. However, input from other people, groups, or situations affect a person's motives.
- Since people act and interact with other people, motivated behavior is often part of a social process.

These basic considerations are fundamental to understanding human behavior. People engage in behaviors that they believe will satisfy their needs. In effect, people are continuously motivated to serve their own interests. This has been referred to as inherent human greed. There is nothing wrong with people serving their own interests so long as the activities they pursue and the behaviors exhibited are legal, moral, and ethical.

Self-Interest and Work

The rewards people seek may be physical, social, psychological, or some combination thereof. With all behavior there are usually some rewards and costs. Rewards are defined as anything that a person views as a benefit. Costs are defined as anything a person views as being detrimental.

Membership in an organization, whether voluntary or compulsory, generally involves some loss of freedom and individuality or other costs. When people join an organization, they have expectations of some rewards from working. When the expected rewards from work are less than the perceived costs, some degree of dissatisfaction will be manifested. Employee dissatisfaction can show itself in numerous ways. The expected rewards from work are not only a function of expectations at the time of hiring, they are also affected by perceived changes in the costs associated with continued employment. The larger the costs, the larger the expected rewards. If the reward is not attainable in the short run, the expectations will increase proportionally with the passage of time. This is similar to an interest charge one would expect to receive if one loaned money today with a promise of repayment at a future date.

When we discuss rewards and costs, it does not mean that one person's reward is at another person's expense. As in a healthy marriage, both parties can profit (rewards are greater than costs) from the relationship. People work for self-serving purposes and organizations hire and retain people for self-serving purposes. Organizations expect people to make a commitment to achieving productivity goals that meld with the organization's overall goal of survival. If organizations are to continue to maintain employees, then employees' contributions must be greater than the costs of their maintenance.

If organizations expect employees to maintain membership and make a high commitment, then an environment must be maintained where employees feel that the rewards exceed the costs. Employees and organizations thus form a symbiotic relationship. The more profitable organizations and employees perceive their relationship, the greater the degree of commitment of both. The same can be said for the relationship between a supervisor and employees. Of course, the reverse also applies. The same can be said from an organizational perspective. The less benefit an organization sees in recruiting and retaining people, the more inclined it will be to substitute machines for people, not make a commitment to employees, and consider relocating to a more hospitable business and/or labor climate. The misunderstanding, or breakdown, of these simple relationships between people and organizations underlies much of the United States' current economic and social problems.

As participants in society, people hold memberships in various types of organizations. Some memberships are voluntary whereas others are somewhat involuntary. Except for those activities or organizations where membership and participation are involuntary, people usually have the choice of withdrawing from participation or membership. Generally speaking, work in business organizations is voluntary. No one can force us to stay at a job. Although people believe they can quit anytime they want, many feel trapped in their jobs. While they do have the option of quitting, it is usually not feasible or even realistic for them to do so. Business conditions, age, family considerations, desire to stay in a community, children in school, and other factors make membership in organizations in the minds of some people more involuntary than voluntary. As long as people feel compelled to maintain membership, they will do so. However, what happens if people feel they are "locked in" to their jobs and the rewards they derive from work are less than the costs? What people tend to do is to change that relationship of rewards and costs.

People seem to have an unlimited capability of finding ways to either reduce the costs and thereby increase the rewards, or increase the rewards and in effect reduce the costs. For example, employees may put less effort into their jobs, be absent more frequently, be careless, or even totally psychologically withdraw from work while being physically present. These are just a few of the ways in which employees can change the proportional relationship between rewards and costs in the work experience. To avoid getting caught, workers individually or in consort use their innate and learned skills. The result is often a hound and fox environment in the workplace. Supervisors spend considerable time and energy trying to catch employees, and employees spend considerable time and energy attempting to divert and elude their supervisor.

Play versus Work

Every supervisor should ask this question: Why is it that for so many people work is work, and for many of these same people play is like work? It is not unusual today to see people putting more time, energy, and money into their leisure activities than into their job-related activities. Golf, tennis, racquetball, jogging, handball, gardening, hunting, and cooking are not exactly what you would call energy-conserving activities. It is also not unusual to see the same people who put so much into their leisure activities putting little time and energy into their jobs. Since leisure or play activities generally do not provide income or job security, and may even threaten employees' ability to maintain their jobs, why do these things occur? Does work provide so few rewards for many that commitments are made to other activities where opportunities for higher rewards exist? Do people's expectations of the rewards from work far exceed the available or possible rewards? Or are activities outside of work so rewarding that jobs cannot provide opportunities for high rewards comparable to the rewards for outside activities? For example, a day at work in a good job in a good company is hard to compare with a sunny day at the seashore or lake, especially if you can be paid for being absent. The answer to the question of why is embodied in all these issues.

In America, people are privileged to have the right, time, and money to belong to diverse organizations and to engage in varied activities. People voluntarily join and maintain membership in organizations and engage in many unorganized activities because the rewards, whether physical, psychological, social, or all three, are greater than the costs. As long as the perceived rewards are greater than the perceived costs, membership and participation will continue. If the rewards and costs were to merge, membership or participation would diminish and eventually terminate. While activities outside the job generally do not provide income, they often provide a high level of physical, psychological, and even social rewards. Perhaps the greatest reward from non-job activities is freedom of choice. In a country where freedom is highly regarded, freedom of choice is an important reward. Other rewards often not available in job-related activities are accomplishment, challenge, and competition.

Rewards and Costs of Work

Not all people want the same things from their jobs, and of course organizations are limited in what rewards they can offer. Some people view jobs as ends in themselves, while others view them as strictly a means to other ends. What people expect in terms of rewards from work is something all levels of management must be aware of. Employees' commitment to their jobs is strictly a function of the rewards expected and received.

Money, because of its versatility, is a convenient reward to give employees. Unfortunately, people's desire for money is relatively insatiable, while all organizations have limits on their abilities to offer it. The optimum objective of any organization and its management must be to create an environment where work is perceived by employees to be play. It must be recognized that for many reasons this desirable goal is often not attainable. It is important to remember that the more employees see work as work, the less of a commitment they will be willing to make and the greater rewards they will expect. It must also be recognized that some needs appear to be insatiable and that many people have developed unrealistically high expectations of the rewards available for working in organizations.

In many organizations, jobs in offices and factories have become highly specialized and narrowly defined. In some cases jobs have become so specialized, simplified, and narrowly defined that reasonably intelligent people with high expectations, when put into them, quickly recognize that those simplistic, mind-deteriorating jobs with no challenge or future will never satisfy the needs they expected to be satisfied partly by work. When jobs fail, partially or totally, to satisfy needs that were expected to be satisfied through work, employees will conclude that the work relationship is unfair and even that they have been cheated. People may then be motivated to keep commitment to their jobs at an absolute minimum and try to derive the maximum from the remaining available rewards, namely, the economic rewards.

Although economic rewards have implicit social and psychological rewards, they can also substitute for desired social and psychological rewards. It is well known that, by conditioning, these substitute satisfiers can become the actual desired rewards. Unfortunately, also by conditioning, money, with all of its economic, social, and psychological meaning, has become the most important reward for workers at lower levels, and increasingly at higher levels in organizations. This is especially true in inflationary times, when expectations cannot be met and existing standards of living are threatened. This situation has created considerable problems for our society. Unionization, inflation, structural unemployment, migration of corporations, higher taxes, higher product costs, poorer product quality, turnover, disciplinary problems, and absenteeism are all related to this situation.

In attempts to satisfy needs, workers may put more emphasis on activities outside of work. From a societal perspective, this has its advantages. However, the degree to which energy and time is spent in activities outside of work at the expense of job-related activities is important. To satisfy needs, workers may also be motivated to retaliate against the organization for what they perceive as its exploitation of them. Retaliation can take place in an infinite number of ways. Even though there is a risk in retaliating against the organization, that is, breaking rules, sabotage, or absenteeism, employees may derive such high levels of satisfaction by engaging in what can be called anti-organizational creativity that they will take the risks.

From the preceding, it should not be interpreted that if organizations could provide jobs and an environment that would satisfy all employees' needs people would cooperate to the fullest degree. First, it would be rare if not impossible for any organization to provide the types of jobs that would satisfy most needs for a majority of employees. Second, needs that are satisfied at one moment may not be satisfied the next moment. Priorities and intensities of people's needs change rapidly. Third, if an organization could create jobs that satisfied all of its employees' needs, employees could become complacent. Supervisors must recognize that by trying to establish the perfect job, environment, and relationships, they could end with employees who may have very high morale but at the same time be nonproductive. Success in dealing with people in organizations lies somewhere between the extremes of creating jobs that provide for the satisfaction of needs but allow for competition, stress, and frustration. In this way, workers will be motivated to seek solutions to problems by working toward organizational goals. What organizations and supervisors do not want to create is an environment where employees perceive that the best way to satisfy needs is to work against organizational goals.

As has been shown, people have diverse needs. Supervisors must develop an assortment of rewards that can be provided to employees who make positive contributions to job requirements. The larger the array of rewards available, the less emphasis will be placed by employees on only one type of reward. Money, especially during periods of inflation when expectations are dimmed and life styles threatened, is important. Contrary to some opinions expressed in management literature, money for most people does not have a middle-to-low level of importance. While money is important as a motivator, it need not be the only one. It is possible to arouse in employees the desire to seek other rewards from work. If the intense emphasis on money can be reduced, all levels of management will have more flexibility. Rewards that could be made available and offered to employees are as follows:

Steady employment
Pleasant and safe working conditions
Good working relationships with others

Interesting job
Challenge
Competition
Recognition
Pride
Sense of accomplishment
Job that contributes to society
Status, prestige
Opportunity to learn a skill or multiple skills
Opportunity to advance
Power
Opportunity to be involved, participate

Every job has its disadvantages. Supervisors must be aware of the costs of work as perceived by employees. As perceived costs rise, expected rewards tend to rise. When expected rewards are not acquired and the costs do not fall, problems occur. Some of the costs of working are as follows:

Loss of opportunity to do something else
Hazardous working conditions
Too much stress
Lack of opportunity to advance
Boring, uninteresting work
Having responsibility for work of others
Having to interact with others
Being overskilled for a job
Being significantly underskilled for a job
Long working hours
Politics
Indefensible discrimination, favoritism
Low pay
Lousy boss
Unfriendly co-workers
Cutthroat competition
No status, prestige, recognition

It is easy to see that costs of work too often exceed the rewards. It is a challenge for supervisors, who often have limited authority to create a climate where employees perceive the rewards as exceeding the costs.

Needs, Motivation, and Jobs

As discussed, in designing jobs and work relationships, organizations unfortunately often end by defining them narrowly, with the result that people are mismatched to jobs and do not have sufficient opportunities for creativity, achievement, or development. Many employees then find they are primarily motivated by money, job security, limited responsibility, and a desire to spend as little time as possible at work, all of which can be viewed as forms of retaliation against the organization. They are lesser forms of retaliation than excessive absenteeism, sabotage, or rule breaking, but they are nonetheless costly to organizations, people, and society. Although money has social and psychological as well as economic meaning, when employees are motivated solely, or for the most part, by money, organizations bear a continually increasing cost burden.

In our materialistic society, money is, and will continue to be, an important incentive for working in organizations. Again, money should not be the single incentive, because the need for money is often insatiable. This condition will push costs upward, unless offset by increased productivity.

Many large organizations, plagued with rising costs, have passed on the increases to the consumer by raising prices. In this way, profit margins are preserved. One of the industries in the United States that has been able to maintain this practice, which in the long run is at society's expense, is the automobile industry. Auto workers, particularly at lower levels, are among the most highly paid, considering wages and benefits, in the nation. They also have considerable legitimate as well as unsanctioned time off. The automobile industry has been plagued by rising labor costs for many years. The industry has attempted to offset high labor costs by massive capital investments in mechanization and automation. They have offset rising labor costs with some success, but the technological gains seem to have reached the point of diminishing returns. The combination of diminishing returns, increasing costs of raw materials, labor, government-imposed costs, and Detroit's attempts to preserve rates of return on investments, makes obvious why automobiles have, in recent years, become very, very expensive. In addition, consumers seem to be willing to accept the rising prices. The automobile industry is just one of the industries in the United States where this condition exists. It has been singled out as an example because of its size and direct impact on the nation's economy.

Many organizations do business in highly competitive markets, or have some limitations on the resources available to the organization. Therefore, they cannot readily pass on increased costs to the consumer. Rising costs, coupled with an inability to offset them, mean declining profit margins. This means less money for growth, replacing worn-out equipment, wages for all employees, and much more. To survive, these organizations must work toward establishing environments and working relationships where maximum cooperation and, in effect, maximum productivity can be achieved at competitive costs. In this way, profits can be maintained for the benefit of all. It is in these organizations, in particular, that supervisors can play a vital role in helping keep labor costs under control. The more dissatisfied employees become with work and work relationships, the more inclined they will be to ask for more in their paychecks—through direct wage increases, uncapped cost-of-living adjustments, or a host of fringe benefits whose costs are often out of control.

If supervisors have the authority, and jobs are not constrained by highly automated equipment or safety or legal needs, then supervisors must develop multiple types of reward systems to satisfy employees' social, psychological, and economic needs. By offering a multiplicity of rewards that satisfy active or activated needs, supervisors will create environments where workers will not put as much emphasis on money.

Depending on their background, experiences, training, personality, values, and physiology, people organize and direct their behavior in an infinite number of ways to satisfy conscious or unconscious needs. What is rational behavior to one person may be totally irrational to another. Behaviors that people engage in may be acceptable to an individual but unacceptable to a group, organization, or society at large. We even see situations where behaviors that people engage in may be acceptable to a group, but unacceptable to an organization or society. People like to believe that they are right when they say or do something. When people rationalize in their own minds that something is right, they will be strongly motivated to repeat the behavior that reinforces the belief.

When supervisors see employees engaging in activities that are in violation of written or unwritten organizational rules and norms, they must take corrective action. Before corrective action can be taken, supervisors must first attempt to identify the reasons why an employee has chosen to behave in a way that, from the organization's or group's viewpoint, is unacceptable. Keep in mind that the employee may see this as proper behavior even though he recognizes that it is against organizational rules or practices.

When a supervisor understands what has motivated an employee to do something, he is halfway toward correcting the problem. The exhibited behavior may be one of fixation, repression, apathy, hostility, projection, aggression, or even violence, but it may also be related to a particular need that is unsatisfied—to the point that the employee has determined that the proper course of action is to achieve a level of satisfaction or to reduce some dissatisfaction. For example, an employee may be motivated to restrict productivity to gain acceptance in a group whose values and norms are anti-organizational. When a supervisor recognizes that the employee is motivated by a need for acceptance by the group, the supervisor can develop strategies that show the employee that the group that will best satisfy his needs over the long run is the organization itself. The organization will provide for the satisfaction of needs if the employee engages in pro-organizational behavior. This may not always be possible, since group pressures are often stronger than organizational pressures. The rewards for conforming to the group's required or expected behavior may exceed the rewards for conforming to organizational requirements. In these situations, supervisors must develop strategies where the rewards for conforming to group norms are reduced and the rewards for conforming to organizational norms are increased. Rewards can include, but should not be limited to the following:

Occasional time off without penalty on attendance records.
Praise and recognition for cooperation.
Promotion to better position.
Stronger consideration for entry into training programs.
Merit increases.
Better job assignments within current classification.
Seeking advice and counsel on work matters.
Preference on overtime distribution.
Delaying or acting quickly to grant requests and address
    complaints.

Job Satisfaction and Dissatisfaction

Employees' dissatisfaction with their jobs or work environment may be evidenced by a variety of positive or negative results. From a positive perspective, frustrated employees may release anxiety and tension by being highly creative and productive. Under these circumstances, organizational goals are met at the highest levels and employees, by releasing tensions, derive satisfaction. It is the satisfaction, or that the anxiety, stress, and tension are released through work that helps to make employees feel psychologically and even physically satisfied. Because of conditioning, it is possible that under certain circumstances some employees will actually feel ill at ease unless a certain amount of frustration and tension is built into their jobs or the work environment. Hence, we see situations where people claim they function best when they are under pressure. Such employees are rare. A supervisor who has them in his unit should strive to create a work environment that generates pressure, which will motivate those employees to seek solutions through creative output.

When employee dissatisfaction results in noncooperative attitudes, low productivity, high absenteeism, extensive griev-ances, complaints about minor issues, equipment sabotage, and other negative behavior, management must look for strategies that either control employee dissatisfaction or chan-nel it into constructive results. If management chooses to con-trol undesirable results of employee dissatisfaction by imple-menting strict organizational controls, such as extensive rules and regulations or hiring more supervisors, it will mean higher costs. Management will usually find that its efforts are at best only partially successful. People have virtually unlimited capabilities for finding solutions to problems. To deal most effectively with employee dissatisfaction, supervisors must look for the underlying causes and determine to what degree they can remove these causes, change employees' perception about the causes, or offer alternative courses of behavior for employees to adopt that will allow them to satisfy other needs. The supervisor may then be able to help an employee to alter a behavior pattern and deal with a need that can be better satisfied and reduce the intensity of an unsatisfied need.

Supervisors must be able to identify the need that motivates an employee to take certain courses of action at a given point in time. Supervisors must ask the question: Are the conditions affecting the level of need deprivation for employees caused by factors within employees themselves, conditions on the job, job relationships, or conditions outside of work? The answer to the question directs supervisors to courses of action for solving the problem.

We have come to understand that in many organizational environments work provides little, if any, satisfaction for em-ployees' needs. Examples of jobs that present no real stimulat-tion, challenge, or opportunity to be creative would be certain clerical jobs, road toll collection, keypunch operation, certain assembly-line jobs, and the like. Unless people in these jobs can satisfy needs outside of work or in other pursuits on the job, they will have needs that will be unsatisfied. To the degree that these needs are unsatisfied, they will serve to be motivators for possible undesirable behavior. For example, an employee working at a boring job who seeks a little stimula-tion, recognition, or excitement at work may obtain satisfaction by causing minor, or even major, disruptions in production or work relationships. If, in such cases, the source of dissatisfaction is inherent in the job the employee may be overqualified, underqualified, or just plain uninterested in the work. Corrective action in the form of a job transfer or changing the job itself would be the appropriate solution to the problem. Under conditions where the job is constrained by technology or safety or legal considerations, supervisors may not be able to change the job activities. When this is not the case, supervisors, if it is within their authority, may be able to change the scope of the job by giving employees more control over what they do, or varying their tasks. In some cases where jobs have been enriched, employees, by having more of a voice in what they do and how they do it, may derive more satisfaction from work. The often used approach of job enrichment, however, is not always successful. In some cases, employees are so conditioned by their job environment that they expect high wages, limited responsibility, and job security as the rewards for as little commitment as possible.

When job enrichment is applied, the supervisor's role changes. Instead of acting as a kind of policeman, the supervisor is compelled to act as a facilitator and coordinator of work—activities that are more in line with the definition of a supervisor's organizational role. In instances where job enrichment has failed, it has often been due to higher management's failure to train supervisors for their new role or supervisors refusing to accept their new role because of perceived losses of status and power.

Another approach supervisors may use to reduce employee dissatisfaction is to rotate employees in a variety of jobs. Rotation can be a formal, sequential process, or informal by means of job bidding and training programs. This approach, known as job enlargement, can help employees derive sufficient satisfaction from their jobs to motivate them to come to work consistently and do a commendable job. When employees are overtrained for their jobs, supervisors can try to place them in stimulating jobs that challenge their abilities and skills. When employees are untrained or underqualified for their jobs, supervisors can initiate training programs or transfer them into jobs more suited to their skills. If organizational conditions permit, supervisors can recommend using flexible working hours, establishing incentive systems, or changing group relationships to reduce problems associated with job dissatisfaction.

Today, it is not unusual to find supervisors setting themselves at a considerable distance and taking limited, if any, interest in their employees' welfare or development. If supervisors are to motivate employees to make high commitments, they must learn to take an ongoing interest in them.

Supervisors must also recognize that when employees do a good job they need some form of approval, or positive reinforcement, of the behaviors they have exhibited. Supervisors must find time to formally and informally recognize employees whose behaviors advance the accomplishment of organizational objectives. Although we all need recognition and praise, and they do not cost anything, a word of caution is necessary. Praise should not be given in a patronizing way; do not praise people as you would your pet dog. And when employees exhibit behavior that is contrary to what is expected, supervisors, before taking punitive action, should counsel employees as to what is expected of them in order to help them help themselves overcome bad habits they may have developed. Taking a sincere interest in the welfare of employees without being paternalistic can reduce many employee-related problems.

Managing Cooperation Problems

Supervisors must develop a sensitivity to informal and formal job relationships that develop among employees. If at all possible, problem employees should not be allowed either to influence new employees or be allowed to work in close proximity to other problem employees. When problem employees interact frequently with one another, they form a cohesive antiorganization group that often coerces and intimidates other employees. If problem employees interact frequently with new employees, they will most assuredly try to influence the new employees' attitudes and behavior. This type of peer pressure can put a new employee, and for that matter any employee, in a stressful position.

Especially in the case of new employees, the reeducational pressures from peers usually motivate them to change and join the problem employees' group, transfer into another job, or quit to avoid the conflict of trying to meet organizational expectations and personal needs while fending off peer pressure. Once employees are reeducated by peers, it is easy for peers to point out how wrong they were, and that the supervisor had been screwing them. Sometimes, as a result, reeducated employees are motivated to retaliate against the supervisor, and even the organization. Supervisors must be sensitive to informal working relationships that evolve, and determine if these relationships are going to work in the best interests of all employees and the organization.

For employee problems that are caused by conditions outside of work, supervisors, or more highly trained specialists in behavior, can take an active part in counseling employees. If necessary, employees can be referred to professionals outside of the organization. It must be remembered that, for the most part, job life and home life are not inseparable, and neither are body and mind. Employees who have problems in their lives outside of work will carry them into work, just as problems that stem from work will be carried outside of work. If an employee's mental or physical state is the underlying cause of a problem on the job, supervisors, by taking time to counsel employees or referring them to other sources for assistance, do themselves, the employee, other employees, and the organization a valuable and necessary service.

All of us at one time or another come face to face with problems that we cannot successfully handle without assistance. People tend to remember how they were treated by others when they were under stress and trying to cope with problems. When supervisors help employees through crises, employees will usually repay the debt many times over because of the positive feelings they will have developed toward their supervisor.

Guidance through counseling can be very effective in helping employees who come to work with poor attitudes and habits, or develop poor habits and attitudes at work, to change their behavior. When "bad" employees go through a change and become "good" employees because of supervisors' reeducation efforts, they often become organization missionaries who are very supportive of the organization and their supervisor.

Supervisors must recognize that people, if handled properly, are valuable assets. This can be the case whether supervisors start with so-called good or bad employees. The result is what is important. However, the cost of the effort involved in changing an employee's behavior must be considered. The objective of any interaction with an employee who has become a problem is to influence the employee to successfully overcome his problem so that he can assume complete job responsibilities. Employees are responsible not only to themselves, but also to supervisors, fellow employees, the organization, family, friends, and society.

When supervisors find that they are unable to deal with causes of employee problems, and the results of the problems or dissatisfactions are negative in terms of work performance or working relationships, then supervisors must apply organizational controls. The process of control is always costly and time consuming and should be, for the most part, a last-resort approach. In cases where employees must be controlled by rules and regulations and systems of discipline, management may be spending more money on problem employees than they are worth to the organization.

It must be remembered that money spent controlling problem employees is money that is taken away from other employees, whose needs should not be ignored because management's attention and resources are directed toward problem employees. Like the child who learns to misbehave to get attention, employees often do the same thing. Employees must be made to understand and accept the fact that when they are given jobs in organizations with the associated rewards, they must accept the many responsibilities that go with the jobs.

If, after sincere efforts have been made, employees cannot accept the responsibilities of membership in the organization, supervisors must be supported in their efforts to terminate their employment. Today, in many organizations, irresponsible employees are maintained at the direct expense of responsible employees. Clearly, if this situation is allowed to persist, the consequences for everyone in our society will be great. It cannot be overemphasized that an organization that engages in the production or delivery of goods or services is not a social welfare agency. Employees today have considerable rights, and they often fail to recognize that with each of these rights, there is a concurrent level of responsibility. With every freedom, privilege, or right there comes one or more responsibilities. Management is a profession where responsibilities always exceed freedoms, privileges, and rights.

Understanding Group Behavior

A group comes into being when a number of people are brought together to perform work or to achieve a common goal. Whether or not they develop into an effective, productive team depends upon many factors. Foremost is that the behavior of a group of employees differs from that of a single employee. Therefore, supervisory skills and techniques that were successful with an individual employee may not achieve the same results when applied to a group of employees.

The ultimate goal of every supervisor is to develop a cohesive work group that is motivated in the fullest sense to achieve organizational objectives as a means of satisfying personal needs and objectives. The benefits of having a work group that is cohesive and pro organization are as follows:

They require less direct supervision.
Peer pressure can be very effective in correcting unacceptable behavior by a member of the group.
Higher productivity often results from a cohesive group of pro organization employees.
Attendance is usually higher.
Quality of work is higher.
Emphasis on money as a single reward is reduced.
Valid input to management on problems is more freely given and tends to be more accurate.

Peer pressures within groups can be formidable, and employees may develop a stronger identification with the group than with the supervisor, or the organization. Every employee who wants to be an accepted member of the group forgoes some individuality and modifies behavior in order to be accorded social position or rank by the group. The stronger an employee's need to be accepted by the group, the more the employee is apt to conform to the group's norms, values, beliefs, and expectations. The employee who places a low priority on acceptance by the group is less apt to be influenced by the group's subtle and direct pressures.

When people work in groups, the politics of human interaction operate continually. Cliques will form because people will be drawn together by common needs and interests. Degrees of likes and dislikes for other group members evolve and various efforts on the part of members of the group to learn other members' strengths and weaknesses will occur.

Through interaction, a definable, yet dynamic social structure will emerge. Traits and characteristics that may be held in high esteem by one group may be held in low esteem by another group. Sometimes what was once held in high esteem by a group can suddenly be held in low esteem by the same group. Group members are accorded social standing or rank based on a number of factors. Some of these factors are:

Physiological characteristics, that is, height, weight, skin tone, color of eyes and hair, gender, age.

Family background, education, experiences.

Organizational title, responsibilities, compensation level, access to information valued by others.

Values, attitudes, political preferences, religious beliefs, spouse's background, ethnic origin.

Ability to help group members meet objectives.

Situational factors.

Existing social structure. The more cohesive the structure, the less opportunity for upward mobility.

The role that any one, or combination, of these factors plays in affecting a person's social position in a group is largely a function of their perceived value by the group's most influential members. When groups are splintered because of internal dissension, the value of traits, characteristics, attitudes, and standards can change rapidly. Also, when groups are splintered, power plays for upward mobility will occur.

Supervisors, if they are to be effective in the long run, must be able to identify the social structure of groups. They must understand how the social structure evolved, how it derives its power to influence members' behavior, and to what degree it changes over time and in different situations. As managers, they should learn techniques and approaches to influence groups either to reinforce the existing social structure or change it.

As stated, there are certain factors that affect a group's according a member social position. On the other side of the coin, people assess groups to determine to what degree they desire acceptance and social position. Their general need for acceptance by other people is one factor. Other factors that people consider are the technical and the social composition of the group. From a technical standpoint, they may have to work with people whose training they consider beneath or above their own level. For example, accountants who are CPA's may not want to associate with bookkeepers. On the other hand, they may want to be associated with them because they would have higher status. Perceptions of the rewards of group membership, whether social, psychological, or economic, determine to what extent people may want to identify with others who have higher or lower status than their own.

The social structure of a group affects members' behavior. The more effort required to acquire high social standing in the group, the less inclined people may be to fight their way up the social ladder. This would not be true, of course, when achieving high social standing is itself a source of high personal satisfaction. If it were difficult to achieve high social position, and that achievement were not important in terms of reward for the employee, the employee would not be inclined to pursue his way aggressively up through the social structure.

Managing the Informal Social Structure

The best way to recognize the informal social structure is to compare it with the formal structure. Supervisors should examine formal working relationships and formal patterns of power, influence, and interaction. By comparing what should be with what actually exists, in terms of influence, interaction, and resultant activities, supervisors can develop a picture of a group's informal social structure. If a supervisor determines that the existing social structure is not serving the best interests of the organization and employees, the supervisor must develop strategies and tactics to change the informal social structure. Some approaches that can be considered are:

- Arranging transfers of group leaders or primary influencers out of the work unit.
- Rearranging formal patterns of interaction by changing jobs, work interaction patterns, or workplace layout.
- Handling employee grievances and the distribution of rewards and punishments. The way supervisors handle employee complaints and give or withhold rewards can enhance and support an existing informal structure, or can create disruption and dissension.
- Cultivating the informal communications system either to create dissension or to reinforce the structure.

When group members, by their own choice, support and enhance the activities of one another, the group becomes a team. If the group is not dominated or controlled by one person or a small group within the larger group, each member, as limited by social standing within the group, is free to exchange ideas, thoughts, and feelings. When an employee derives satisfaction from being part of a team, this becomes one of the rewards for employment in the organization. In cases where employees derive multiple rewards from work, they are less inclined to change jobs, even if another job offers a higher level of compensation. Up to a point, satisfaction of social and psychological needs can be an effective substitute compensator for money. There is usually some point, however, where the money differential is so great that other rewards are insufficient to retain the employee.

Supervisors may find the following guidelines helpful in establishing a work group that is cohesive and pro organization:

- Understand the group's informal social structure.
- Be aware of employee needs and attempt to create an environment that facilitates direct satisfaction of needs or acceptable substitute satisfiers.
- Give recognition and praise on the basis of merit.
- Distribute other rewards or corrective action according to merit. Merit must be carefully defined, and employees must have the right to question, without personal risk, the distribution or withholding of rewards.
- Be approachable on problems and flexible in leadership style.
- Establish work climates that are ego enhancing and contribute to a desire on the part of employees to cooperate.
- Have realistic expectations of employees and establish relationships of mutual trust and confidence.
- Stand up for employees when they are right and help them learn from mistakes when they are wrong.
- Let employees know what is expected of them and give feedback on performance.
- Take a sincere interest in employee welfare and development.
- Create a team identity by rotating job assignments among personnel. In this way, people lose some of the parochialism associated with claimed ownership of a particular job. They see themselves as being part of a team with varying responsibilities.
- Develop group attitudes, norms, and influences that center on cooperative teamwork and the reduction of antagonistic functions.
- Develop a team spirit and a desire among employees to compete as a team instead of as individuals.

A word of caution is in order. The group, while being cohesive and strong, should not become so strong as to suppress individual identities. People must retain their individualism while recognizing that they are part of a team. This is a very difficult and delicate balance to achieve and maintain.

Within any group, one or more informal leaders will emerge. The leaders are important to both the supervisor and the group's members. The informal and formal organizations are, to a degree, in competition for the employees' loyalty. Effective supervisors can identify the power structure within the group, and they also know how to manage relationships so all concerned benefit. Informal group leaders are key people because they are powerful influencers of others' behavior. Informal group leaders emerge because they represent the values, beliefs, feelings, and attitudes of group members; they are effective communicators; they are trusted, and high confidence is placed in their opinions and judgments; they best help group members satisfy their needs; and they are supported by other key members of the group.

Informal group leaders may possess many of the traits, abilities, and characteristics of supervisors. While they lack formal organizational recognition and formal status, they must be recognized by the formal power structure because their feelings and opinions carry more weight, or generate more concern, than the feelings and opinions of others.

Employees are often more loyal to the informal leadership in the organization than to the formal leadership. In these cases, the informal leaders are in a position to influence group behavior significantly. While they can influence behavior, if they speak or act outside the acceptable limits of their role as perceived by the group, their leadership position is weakened. The more secure their position, the broader their operating limits. However, since in any group there is competition for the leadership role, a competitor can quickly take advantage of a situation where the incumbent leadership becomes vulnerable.

The primary members of a group are those who are most closely aligned with the leadership. If the group is cohesive, the primary members are the emissaries and staunch political supporters of the leaders. In a sense, they form the executive committee of the group. The third stratum is composed of the secondary members, who range from those close to the primary members down to the group deviates and isolates. The lower a person's social rank, the less influence he is likely to have over the others in the group.

A work group tends to reflect a common set of desires that may or may not be evident from observation. The common threads in a group are:

- The desire to satisfy members' needs for social interaction.
- The need to control the actions of the group's members by establishing acceptable norms—rewarding members who act as expected and punishing those who do not.
- A need to protect individual members through collective representation.
- The desire to exercise greater influence over work and the work environment through group interaction.
- The desire to enhance group effectiveness, be it pro or antiorganization, by pooling individual talents and resources.

No supervisor should underestimate the degree of pressure that an informal group's political structure can exert upon other employees and the formal organizational structure. Research has shown that employees may fear group pressure far more than they fear organization pressure. The same applies to the evaluation of rewards. Many workers value the rewards given by their peer group more than the rewards given by the formal organization.

In terms of the dynamics of groups, it must be remembered that positions of leadership are not formally defined by job descriptions. They are based on status, power, and the ability to influence. Supervisors must learn to recognize the attitudes, values, aspirations, and degree of influence that the social power structure of a group can exert. Supervisors who do not learn to recognize and manage a group's power structure will never achieve the same level of effectiveness as supervisors who do. A group's social power structure can be an asset to the supervisor, or it can be a liability. Unless a supervisor wants to break up a social structure, it is usually better to try to develop a cohesive pro organization structure so that the group's leaders can act as de facto assistants to the supervisor.

When the informal power structure of a group has cohesiveness and solidarity and is aligned with organizational objectives, members who stray from their formal, or informal, responsibilities, required behavior, and objectives are apt to be the recipients of double discipline. They face the possibility of being formally disciplined by their supervisor as well as their peers, and discipline from one's peers can be more severe than that administered by the formal organization.

Effective Working Relationships and Employee Safety

Safety in the workplace is more of a problem in factories than in offices. However, many offices have equipment that presents some of the same potential dangers as the equipment in factories. Safety is a responsibility of all members of management and all employees. While it is impossible to make a factory or an office a fail-safe environment, supervisors must be aware of practices or operations that are, or could be, safety hazards. Supervisors must communicate their concern for safety to all employees and must be open minded to employee input on safety problems.

Injured or sick employees are liabilities to their employers, co-workers, family, friends, and society. An employee who is injured on the job receives worker's compensation, sickness and accident benefits, some other payment of salary, and most medical expenses, all, in effect, paid for directly or indirectly by the employer. In addition, the employer loses the services of the injured or sick employee.

Co-workers of injured employees may perceive the workplace as being more dangerous than it actually is, and may express their concern in a number of potentially negative ways. They may also perceive that management is not concerned about safety in the workplace, and that perception can manifest itself in poor work attitudes and losses in productivity and profits.

In many cases safe practices are matters of common sense. Supervisors must learn to recognize existing or potential hazards in the workplace and that certain employees may be more accident prone than others; even normally cautious employees may not always be fully cognizant of the dangers around them. This can be especially true when employees become conditioned to working in a dangerous environment; they often take too many things for granted.

Employees in factories, particularly in their orientation period, must be made aware that a factory can be dangerous to work in if safety practices and rules are not followed. Untrained employees must not be permitted to do jobs that require training in handling potentially dangerous equipment or material. This can be a real problem in a unionized organization. Labor-management agreements with seniority, job-bidding, temporary transfer, and bumping clauses may give employees the right to work in jobs that they should not be allowed to work in. In a unionized organization, the union's support of safety in the workplace must be actively encouraged; the union should support management's actions, including the reduction of work hazards or discipline of employees who do not follow safety practices and procedures.

The same applies, but usually to a lesser degree, in offices. With the implementation of technically sophisticated equipment in offices, many dangers that did not exist in the past are present today. Office workers tend to be less sensitive to the dangers of the workplace than factory workers. In these cases, supervisors should make a special effort to alert employees to safety practices. All organizations must develop safety rules, and employees must be told why the rules are necessary and the consequences of violating them. Supervisors must ensure that the rules or guidelines are followed.

It is generally advisable for organizations, whether or not unionized, to appoint an employee safety committee to work with supervisors and others in reviewing safety practices in the workplace. Separate committees may be established for different types of work areas and should meet periodically with supervisors and others, such as personnel specialists, to discuss safety needs and concerns.

In cases where safety or health hazards exist, corrective action should be taken as quickly as possible. When the degree of danger is disputed, the costs of changing operations or installing protective devices on equipment may be so great as to make operations unprofitable. The facts should be openly discussed with safety committee members. A decision to remain profitable and not take corrective action must be weighed against employees' reactions and the actual dangers that are involved.

A position taken by management on a safety matter should be communicated in entirety to employees. Safety issues can easily become emotional. Whenever employees question management's decision regarding safety, supervisors should be sensitive to the employees' reasons for questioning. One reason for paying attention to employees' concerns about safety is that the employees, with complete immunity, can lodge complaints with the state or federal offices responsible for enforcement of safety laws. Another reason is that employees often see safety problems in a workplace that supervisors or others do not fully recognize or appreciate. Supervisors who do not express concern about safe practices communicate the feeling that they are more concerned about production than employee welfare. Supervisors who express concern about safety and require that safe practices be maintained gain the confidence and trust of their employees. This, as has been discussed, goes a long way in helping to build cooperative work relationships.

With the enactment of the federal Occupational Safety and Health Act (OSHA) and state laws that complement OSHA, government has become increasingly concerned about the mentally and physically debilitating aspects of working life. Organizations are permitted to do business with society because they are perceived to serve legitimate social purposes and function in ways that are acceptable to society. An organization that continually runs counter to society's values, feelings, or expectations runs the risk of losing customers, being forced out of existence, or being put under society's control by means of regulation.

It can be said that to some extent industry brought on itself the passage of federal and state laws pertaining to safety and health in the workplace. It can also be said that some government employees, at all levels, are antibusiness and often over-zealously apply the law. The key to handling relationships with government authorities is to educate them on the realities of work environments. On occasion, it may be necessary to challenge their decisions. Some of the problems that existed in the past have diminished somewhat, in part because of maturing relationships between government and business.

Supervisors should not let safety in the workplace become a political issue. Unfortunately, some workers use the issue of safety for political gain. They will threaten and intimidate supervisors by reporting to government agencies and alleging unsafe practices by the organization. This could launch an investigation with all of its concomitant problems.

Sometimes employees will claim that a job is dangerous in order to avoid having to do it. When employees challenge supervisors' decisions, the burden of proof is usually on the supervisor. However, when employees contend that an operation is unsafe, the burden of proof shifts to the employees. Supervisors must be careful to determine whether an employee is using safety for political purposes or really believes that a job or operation is unsafe. In other words, an employee may sincerely believe that an activity is unsafe and refuse to comply with a supervisor's directive, when in fact the activity is safe. In these instances, supervisors will find it in their best interests to respect the employee's feelings. However, when a supervisor is convinced that an employee is using safety for political purposes, or to avoid doing a job, the supervisor cannot support the employee.

Sometimes employees will feign or distort an injury or illness to get out of work. They may even stay away from work and collect compensation for the feigned injury or illness. If employees who adopt these practices are allowed to get away with them, it shows a weakness in management's ability to handle problems. This weakness will have an eventual debilitating effect on other employees' attitudes and desire to cooperate. Although supervisors must be very careful in contesting an employee's claims of illness or injury, they must, nonetheless, do so when they feel it is necessary. In handling these situations, an in-depth knowledge of the employee and his past behavior and motives is a necessity. If a supervisor is unfamiliar with an employee's normal behavior, it is difficult, if not impossible, to properly judge whether or not the employee is exaggerating an illness or injury.

Supervisors are also obligated to set the example for others to follow. By setting good examples and enforcing organizational safety practices and rules, they establish and reinforce a climate of concern for employee welfare. Swift and decisive corrective action against employees who cannot, or will not, conform to safety practices and rules demonstrates to other employees the supervisor's commitment to maintaining safety. Safety in the workplace is an important aspect of all employees' needs for security. Remember, when an employee's need is satisfied, it no longer serves as an active motivator.

3

Selecting, orienting, and training employees

THE supervisor's role in recruitment of employees has been purposely deleted from this chapter because in most organizations supervisors have limited input into the recruitment process, which is usually assigned to personnel specialists. On occasion, however, supervisors play a direct role in the recruitment of highly skilled employees.

In many organizations, supervisors have little, if any, real input into the selection process either. This practice is an organizational travesty. Personnel specialists, no matter how good their intentions, do not always have sufficient knowledge of the jobs for which they are required to obtain employees. Supervisors know more about the jobs under their direction and are in a better position to review applicants. While supervisors may not have the same level of training and experience as personnel specialists in the various dimensions of the selection process, they certainly recognize that the person hired must fit the job and the organization and be able to get along with other people. The cost of recruiting, especially of highly skilled employees, has risen sharply in recent years. Scarcity of people to fill many skilled jobs is commonplace. Considerable resources are wasted when the wrong person is hired for a job, or the right person is hired and placed in the wrong job. If organizations took the time to calculate the real costs of poor recruitment, selection, and placement practices, awareness of those costs would be sufficient incentive for management to change procedures and practices.

When people are hired, the costs of maintaining them as new employees usually exceed the benefits derived from their services; it takes time to learn how to do a job well in a new job environment. Poor personnel practices only lengthen the payback period. Other results of poor personnel practices that have received a lot of attention in the media and the courts are the costs of lawsuits filed by employees for almost unlimited reasons, actions by government agencies, and organizing efforts by unions.

When people are hired without proper selection screening and remain employed beyond a probationary period, they often exhibit a higher probability of becoming problem employees. Whether they are represented by a union or are protected by antidiscrimination legislation, most employees have considerable job rights once they have completed a prescribed probationary period. Most supervisors recognize how difficult it is to discharge an unsatisfactory employee, particularly if the employee has accrued seniority.

Organizations must decide whether they want to spend money on careful recruitment and selection, so that only the best are hired, or whether they want to hire anyone who walks in the door and then spend time, money, and energy taking disciplinary action against problem employees. In organizations where unions represent employees, employers can and often do find themselves in arbitration proceedings as the result of poor recruitment, selection, orientation, or placement practices. Employees, whether they have union representation or not, have civil rights laws under which to seek protection from employers. The costs to organizations and society of poor personnel practices, especially the costs associated with trying to discharge problem employees, are astronomical. Too often they have been accepted as just another cost of doing business. In many instances, the costs and efforts required are so great that employers resign themselves to living with unsatisfactory employees. All supervisors recognize the long-term results of having to live with problem employees in their unit. Higher levels of management, who are to a degree insulated from day-to-day problems, are at times unsympathetic to the personnel problems of supervisors.

It is essential that supervisors formally participate in the selection, orientation, and placement process. An organization that does not include supervisors, or other employees, in the selection process loses an opportunity for valuable input. The more people with different perspectives who participate in the selection process, the higher the probability that the correct selection will be made. Even though many instruments and techniques are available to help measure the traits, characteristics, and abilities of potential employees, the interview process is still the technique that carries the greatest weight in the selection process.

Unfortunately, even the organizations that allow supervisors to participate in the process do not allow them sufficient time to interview applicants. The arguments advanced for not allowing supervisors sufficient time to interview are usually: (1) We can't afford to have the supervisor away from the work or the work area, (2) It's too expensive, (3) It's too time consuming. These defensive arguments are unacceptable when the costs of poor selections are considered. This is the classic case of being penny wise and dollar foolish.

Interviewing Techniques

In the selection process, two approaches are most frequently used in interviewing: directive and nondirective interviews. A directive interview is a technique whereby the interviewer has outlined in advance specific questions to be answered and guides the interview by asking the applicant the directed questions. The advantage of this type of interview is that the interviewer, working from a predeveloped list of questions, makes certain that all information required for selection evaluation is obtained. Unnecessary information is not solicited. The disadvantage of this approach is that the interview is too structured, and the interviewer tends to be more concerned with asking questions than listening to answers. In addition, structured interviews tend to cause anxiety in applicants. Applicants are apt to respond more to what they think the interviewer wants to hear than to say what they are really thinking.

The nondirective interview is an unstructured approach in which broad, general questions are asked so that the applicant may openly discuss needs, goals, feelings, and attitudes. A nondirective interview attempts to find out how and what the person being interviewed feels and thinks. The basic approach of the nondirective interview is to encourage applicants to openly communicate. Nondirective interviews are more difficult to conduct than directive interviews. They require interviewers to guide conversations while being effective listeners. Interviewers must exert self-control and withhold their own ideas and feelings while conducting a nondirective interview, and they should avoid expressing approval or disapproval even though an applicant may request it. This can be exasperating, but it is necessary because a more complete picture of the applicant is usually obtained by this approach. Because it is a difficult method to use effectively, considerable training of interviewers is necessary. For this reason, organizations often prefer to have supervisors who participate in the selection process use the directive approach.

An effective approach is the combined directive-nondirective interview, which combines the best features of both. When using this method, interviewers solicit responses from a broad list of questions and allow applicants wide latitude in responding. When applicants stray beyond the perimeters of a question or topic, interviewers guide them back to the main track. It is a good technique because it requires responses to specific questions that have been identified as being important to the selection decision. The questions are not asked in a structured fashion or predetermined sequence, and the applicant is given latitude in responding. This approach tends to reduce an applicant's anxiety and tension. It requires less skill and training on the part of the interviewer than the nondirective approach because it is partially structured.

Preparing for an Interview

Because many supervisors who participate in the selection process are not trained to prepare and conduct interviews, they often do a less than satisfactory job. Any interview situation produces tensions and anxieties in interviewers and applicants. The objective of the interview, for both the interviewer and the applicant, is to mutually examine one another in as open a manner as possible. In this way, each can decide whether to offer or accept a position. In what, even under ideal conditions, amounts to a rather short period of time, a lot must be accomplished, with a minimum of costly mistakes.

As in a football game, a lot of preparation must take place before going onto the field, that is, the interview session. Unlike a football game, where one team wins and the other loses, in the selection process both sides should come out eventual winners. Following are some suggested guidelines for preparing for and conducting a successful interview.

• Establish an interview game plan. Determine in advance what general and specific information is needed to help make an intelligent decision about the applicant. Develop an itinerary if others are to participate in the process, and communicate the game plan and itinerary to them on a need-to-know basis.

• Keeping in mind the job requirements, the law, and the applicant's right to privacy, as much information as possible should be secured and reviewed before the interview takes place. Care must be exercised in not drawing too many conclusions about an applicant's character, experiences, skills, strengths, and weaknesses before an interview. In general, the more you know about an applicant before an interview, the easier it will be to establish rapport. Again, the danger in knowing too much in advance is that the applicant may be prejudged. Always remember that, especially in interviewing, first impressions spill over and often end as the final impressions. There is nothing ruder or more improper than reading over an applicant's profile, reference letters, or other material while the applicant is sitting in your office. This communicates that you really do not care about the person; otherwise you would have read the materials before the interview.

• Keep in mind that the interview is an opportunity for mutual exploration. Unless a stress type of interview is planned, do not add to what is already a stress-producing situation. Physical setting for an interview is just as important as mental setting. Before conducting the interview, establish the physical environment. Privacy and some degree of comfort are necessary for a good interviewing climate. Try to conduct the interview in a private area, and try to avoid any interruptions; if that is impossible, keep them to a minimum. Hold off telephone calls and interruptions by supervisors, peers, and employees, unless it is an emergency. Frequent interruptions create about the same type of image as reading applicants' references in front of them.

• Have available nonconfidential information about the organization, its history and products, that the applicant will need to know or may inquire about. Anticipate the applicant's questions in advance of the interview to assist you in preparing your information base.

Conducting a Successful Interview

Training and advance preparation reduce the risk of failing to conduct a successful interview. One of the first things to do is to put the applicant at ease. This can readily be accomplished by creating a somewhat informal atmosphere. Dress, use of titles, room setting, and seating arrangement can be used to create any range of climates. A firm handshake, clean appearance, clear articulate speech, and looking at the person are just as important for a supervisor conducting an interview as they are for the applicant.

Too many supervisors make the mistake of believing that interviewing is a one-way process and that the burden of worthiness is entirely on the applicant. Many an applicant has turned down a position offer, or has been turned off during an interview, because of poor impressions received. A brief introductory conversation about a hobby or interest of the applicant can start the applicant talking and establish rapport. Even talking about the weather can be used. Offering nonalcoholic beverages can help establish a good climate.

Interviewers and applicants must consider the short as well as the long run. "Is this a person who can grow and make contributions to the organization?" would be a concern of the interviewer. "Is this a place where I can pursue my career?" would be a concern of the applicant. Although we live in a highly mobile society, the fact that people and organizations often establish long-term relationships cannot be overlooked. All things considered, organizations and employees usually benefit from long-term relationships.

Supervisors must have some knowledge of the history, traditions, growth, and future of the organization. In the course of the interview, the supervisor should attempt to learn about the applicant's short- and long-term career aspirations. Short-term goals and aspirations are particularly important in considering whether the position that the applicant is being interviewed for will fit his needs and goals.

Supervisors should be familiar with equal opportunity and fair employment practices and make certain that they do not ask questions that would be in violation of the law. In today's legal climate, information that is necessary to the selection process often cannot be obtained by specific questions. Supervisors must develop ways of asking questions pertinent to the selection that cannot be asked directly. Today's restrictive legal climate is another reason why many organizations do not allow supervisors to participate in the interview process. The fear is that supervisors who are not as knowledgeable of the law as personnel specialists will ask questions that can get the organization in trouble. Training, of course, can reduce this concern.

As noted, as much time as necessary should be taken to get information about the applicant. This is especially true when the position is one of responsibility and the wrong person in the job can cost the organization a lot of money. The higher the level of the position for which the applicant is being considered, the more time should be spent learning about the applicant. The applicant should also have sufficient time to learn about the organization and the job for which he is being considered. The worst thing that can happen is to bring into a job a new employee who has relocated from another part of the country and for the organization or the employee to find out a poor choice was made. It is advisable to give an applicant who is being seriously considered for a position a tour of the facilities and introductions to other employees. Having managers, personnel specialists, and some of your best employees interview the applicant is beneficial to all, as it gives them the opportunity to view one another from varying perspectives. Itineraries are useful although rigid time schedules should not be set.

Applicants should also be informed about organization policies, practices, and compensation structure, including performance evaluation systems and procedures. Organizations tend to go to great lengths to put the best foot forward during the interview process. Applicants have a tendency to do the same. In the long run it is better for all parties to be as honest as possible.

Many organizations find it to everyone's benefit to interview the applicant's spouse. With more career-oriented spouses, this is becoming increasingly important. A spouse who cannot pursue his or her career, or a spouse or children who have difficulty in adapting to a new community can, and often do, cause problems for new employees. This spillover effect of job and home life can be very troublesome.

It is also advisable to arrange to dine with an applicant who looks promising. There is something equalizing about people eating together, and many communication barriers dissolve over a good meal. Considerable information about people in organizations can be learned during a breakfast, lunch, or dinner.

Joining an organization is not that different from getting married. The more unpleasant surprises you find out about your spouse after you are married, the higher the probability that the marriage will not last. The same can be said about jobs.

When interviewing an applicant, it is especially important to take mental notes. Some people have a habit of writing down impressions about an applicant while the person is being interviewed. Taking notes while interviewing will increase the applicant's anxiety and apprehension. The applicant might lose interest in the job in an attempt to figure out what is being written and whether or not a favorable impression is being made. The proper approach is to take mental notes. When the interview is concluded and the applicant has left the room, mental notes should be written out in detail. This should be done even if the applicant is not going to be offered a job. Under present law, applicants who are turned down for jobs can file complaints. The burden of proof for refusing a job to an applicant rests with the organization, not the applicant.

Written notes should be reviewed to finalize impressions of the applicant. If many people are being interviewed for a position, the various sets of notes about applicants can be reviewed to help determine who is the best person for the position, and why an offer of employment should be extended.

When an interview is completed, the applicant should be advised that either the interviewer or someone else from the organization will be in touch and how long it will take to be contacted. Many organizations take much too long to follow up on an applicant, or do not follow up at all. Supervisors should also learn what constraints applicants are under in terms of needing a job or having job offers from other organizations. Of course, the date of the applicant's availability for work must be ascertained.

Dangers to Be Avoided in Interviewing

People have selective ways of interpreting what they hear. Supervisors, like other people, have beliefs, feelings, and ideas about everyone else and the world. Supervisors must be careful to retain their objectivity when they interview. Some things that should be avoided in assessing an applicant are:

The so-called halo effect. We have a tendency to identify with and relate more to people who are like us physically, psychologically, and socially than to people who are different from us in any respect. To the extent that people are different, our preferences, biases, or prejudices often affect our objectivity. For example, a supervisor may like or dislike a particular minority, and an applicant in that minority group may cause a supervisor to be consciously, or unconsciously, biased for or against the applicant. However, in selecting employees supervisors must consider the extent to which applicants who are different from others in the group will be accepted by the group. Obtaining employees who will fit into the organization and the unit and remaining in compliance with the variety of fair employment practices and equal opportunity laws and regulations can be a difficult problem. Supervisors are morally, ethically, and legally obligated to take some risks in hiring employees in order to be in compliance with the spirit and letter of the law.

Making generalizations from what has been seen or heard. Supervisors may overgeneralize from a statement the applicant made or from something they observed. For example, the interviewer may conclude from an evasive answer that there is something unflattering in the applicant's background. The applicant may not be dressed in the latest style of clothing. In checking the applicant's background, someone who was contacted may not have given an unqualified endorsement of the applicant. Or a letter of reference may have been totally honest in discussing the applicant's weaknesses and could prejudice judgments. There is some evidence to indicate that reference letters may not reflect an applicant's real qualities and qualifications.

On the other hand, because it is difficult to remove employees once they are employed beyond a defined probationary period, and the law often prevents asking some job-related questions, conclusions must be drawn from the limited information obtained in the interview. It is usually better for supervisors, especially if they are experienced, to act on what they perceive, if facts indicating otherwise do not exist. In other words, if a supervisor hears or sees certain things about the applicant that arouse concern, it is better to be safe than sorry.

Hiring people who are significantly overqualified for a job. Some supervisors believe that the applicant with the highest qualifications, which may far exceed the job requirements, is the best person to hire. A person who is overqualified for a job often becomes bored and ends as a problem employee unless he can be given challenging assignments or be placed in a more challenging job.

Hiring people who are significantly underqualified for a job. If an employee, after training and reasonable time for adjustment, cannot be a contributing member of the group, problems with the employee and others will evolve. This condition has been a real problem for supervisors and organizations in instances where voluntary or involuntary compliance with civil rights laws are concerned. The only viable solution for avoiding problems involving underqualified people is to not hire them, or establish meaningful remedial training programs prior to placement, followed by training once on the job. The author strongly endorses the concept of remedial training instead of not hiring people. Organizations and supervisors who maintain separate, lower standards of performance for underqualified employees do not benefit anyone, least of all the employees labeled as not being expected to perform up to everyone else's level.

Overcomparison with current employees. While a new employee must fit into the work group, it would be unrealistic to hire people who all came from similar social, economic, cultural, racial, or religious backgrounds. Our nation is made up of people from many different backgrounds. The composition of an organization's work force should, considering the types of skills employed and labor market availability, reflect the composition of the community and the market served. The benefits of having a work force composed of people from differing backgrounds far exceeds the disadvantages.

Orienting New Employees

The old saying that first impressions are often lasting impressions is especially appropriate to new employees. Most readers can remember the first few days on some of the jobs they held during their lives. Those first few days were often filled with concern, anxiety, apprehension, and curiosity. If no one took time to reduce those concerns and to make one feel part of the group, those initial feelings tended to remain for a long time. Some even left permanent scars. If a new employee gets off to a bad start, he often never recovers. A program for orienting new employees is not a luxury activity, it is an absolute necessity. The primary objective of any orientation program is to facilitate new employees fitting into their jobs, work groups, the organization, and even the community. Unfortunately, many organizations have no orientation program for new employees, and many of those that have them allow supervisors to play only a limited role. The primary responsibility for orientation usually rests with personnel specialists. That is wrong. The primary responsibility should be with supervisors. Personnel specialists should assist supervisors, not the opposite.

Orientation is not a one-shot activity for new employees. It should not be limited to reviewing a simple checklist of necessary information to be communicated. When new employees are properly oriented, the probability of problems occurring with them is considerably lessened. A complete orientation program could last over a period of six months to a year.

Orientation starts even before a new employee reports for the first day of work. When new hires or transfers are relocating geographically, the organization and supervisors should provide assistance with the relocation. Anyone who has relocated has experienced the problems associated with housing, shopping, schools, physicians, dentists, conformance with laws and much more. Supervisors should be in contact with new employees before they report for the first day of work. It is essential that the people with whom a new employee will interface be informed about the new employee. They should be encouraged to help the new employee through the adjustment period.

Whether or not a formal orientation program exists, supervisors should be knowledgeable about the organization's history, products, services, philosophy, traditions, practices, standard operating procedures, opportunities, and benefits. To facilitate the flow of information, it is advisable for supervisors to work from a checklist and to have available all printed information about the organization. Just handing written material to new employees is insufficient; it must be explained to them.

The orientation process should have these objectives:

- To help new employees develop favorable impressions of the organization, their jobs, and fellow workers.
- To facilitate satisfying new employees' needs for security and acceptance.
- To minimize the development of problems at the outset and in the future.

The following guidelines may prove helpful to supervisors in orienting new employees. The guidelines would, of course, be modified for each operating environment.

- Introduce new employees to their co-workers.
- Secure the tools, equipment, uniforms, and passes that employees will need to do their jobs.
- Make the employees knowledgeable about their jobs and your expectations in terms of performance.
- Give the employees essential information about the organization and its products or services.
- Give employees a tour of the facility or plant.
- See that employees know where the time clock is located, if they are required to use one. Inform them about lunch areas, rest rooms, and parking areas.
- If the organization has an employee handbook, review its contents with them. If your organization does not have an employee handbook, all personnel policies and procedures that would normally be in a handbook should be communicated and thoroughly discussed.
- Schedule follow-up discussions. It is important to recognize that new employees will be overwhelmed by all of this information. There will be things that have been missed, forgotten, incorrectly understood, or not fully covered during the orientation. Supervisors must show a genuine concern for new employees in terms of their fitting into the job and job environment.
- Employees should be informed of the general job rights they have. This is especially important for complaint handling or grievance procedures. New employees must be informed about the organization's fringe benefits and what these benefits

are worth. They should know how to utilize such benefits as medical insurance, disability, and worker's compensation, if they should ever be needed.

• If the organization is unionized, new employees should be informed of their duties and obligations to the union. They should get a copy of the current labor-management agreement and should be introduced to the union steward or committeeman in their work area. Supervisors should not give personal views about the union, but simply see that employees are oriented to the union and its role in the organization.

• Schedule follow-up meetings. Do not wait for employees to report that they are having problems. Learn to recognize potential or existing problems and take action to correct them quickly. If employees do not meet expectations, find out why, and take rehabilitative or corrective action promptly.

Employee Training and Development

Many people tend to use the terms training and development interchangeably. The difference between the terms is important to understand. Training programs related to jobs emphasize the learning of knowledge and skills necessary to achieve and maintain an acceptable level of performance. Development goes beyond training; it does not focus on skill development, although skill development is implicit. Rather, it focuses on growth and improvement of employees as members of the organization and as human beings. The payoffs from employee development come over the long run, while the payoffs for training alone tend to be for the short run.

To survive over time, organizations must remain responsive to the needs of employees, as well as the needs of customers. Employees' needs can be served only if the organization is effectively and efficiently serving customer needs. We live in a world of continuous change. As things change, people and organizations must also change. This means that jobs and relationships in organizations must change to best facilitate meeting objectives.

The organization that attempts to cling to the past when

society, or the markets served, perceives that things should be otherwise, will become part of the past. Implicit in the ability to change is the necessity for developing a flexible, adaptive work force. People must not only be trained in certain skill areas, they must also have a broad enough base of knowledge so that when conditions or events require it, they can rapidly learn new skills or adapt to new situations. People must also learn how to adjust and adapt to differing sets of relationships that are brought about as a result of change. From an employee perspective, training and development help to satisfy, among other needs, those for self-esteem, economic security, socialization, achievement.

Organizations that can correctly forecast change and adapt with rapidity and accuracy will be those that will survive and prosper over the long run. The organizations that go out of business or are bought out by others at distress prices are those that could not successfully adjust and adapt.

Training and development activities must be integrated with short- and long-range planning. To meet the broad objectives of training and development, specific types of training must be identified. Induction training, new techniques, equipment and processes training, remedial training, technological displacement training, apprenticeship training, and rehabilitative training are some of the types of programs. Within any of these programs, three interrelated objectives must be met. The first is to develop within trainees the proper technical skills, such as equipment operation and motor skills, so that trainees can safely perform jobs with proficiency and efficiency. The second objective is to develop within trainees the body of facts, ideas, concepts, methods, and procedures to enable them to visualize mentally and physically what it is they must do and why it must be done. If trainees can develop an understanding of the relationship of the job elements and the relationship of their job to other jobs, the probability of the trainees mastering jobs and making a commitment to doing their jobs well is increased. When trainees understand more than the mechanics of a job, they are better able to solve nonroutine job problems. They are also better able to creatively change the job to maintain peak performance.

The third objective of training is to help trainees to develop proper work and interpersonal relationship attitudes. Proper attitudes are communicated not just by what is said, but by what is practiced. Supervisors can talk about safety, but if they do not practice safety, employees will develop the wrong conclusions about supervisors' concern for their welfare. Also, employees themselves may begin to treat safety as being unimportant.

Many other benefits from training accrue for supervisors, employees, and organizations. When supervisors participate in training employees, they interact with employees and therefore get to know them better. They learn more about employees' needs, wants, concerns, aspirations, and potentials. Supervisors who participate in the development of employees and who perform their jobs effectively and efficiently help further their own careers as managers. The supervisor who develops a highly productive, cohesive work group is a strong candidate for raises and promotions.

Trained employees, if committed to achieving organizational goals, are more self-reliant and self-confident, and require less controlling supervision. Trained employees usually are more conscientious and take more pride in what they do. Insecure and unconscientious employees often end by becoming problem employees because they are motivated to protect themselves by hiding their own insecurities and inefficiencies. Supervisors who do not have to spend the better part of the work day watching and controlling employees have more time to manage.

For employees, the advantages of training are many. Trained employees have a higher probability of not only succeeding in their current jobs, but also in their careers. Trained employees who take pride in their work produce more, and that in itself satisfies a variety of needs. Trained employees who develop a strong self-image, as long as they are in jobs that provide some challenge, generally develop pro-organization attitudes. They are absent from work less frequently, file fewer grievances, and are less apt to engage in overt and covert activities intended to retaliate against the organization. When organizational costs are lower, employees' job security, opportunity for advancement, and money available for wage increases are all higher.

For organizations, the benefits are numerous. A trained work force is more efficient and more effective. Since it is more productive, their costs are apt to be lower than competitors whose workers are not trained. Therefore, profits tend to be higher. Profits can be redistributed or retained for continued expansion and growth. Trained workers who develop the ability to assimilate new knowledge quickly can be a ready source of internal manpower to fit the organization's growth needs. When organizations cannot properly utilize the skills of trained employees, the probability of losing those employees to competitors increases. No organization wants to train employees for the competition.

In today's competitive markets, an organization cannot afford to stand still for very long. To stop moving is to sow the seeds of self-destruction. Organizations must plan for future needs and continually develop employees to fit changing needs. An outstanding example of such an organization is the International Business Machines Corporation. IBM has grown rapidly, pays high wages, has excellent job security, offers opportunity for advancement, and, overall, has an adaptive, cohesive, pro-organization work force and has been very profitable for many years. IBM dominates its industry and has continued to grow for over two decades.

Planning Employee Training Programs

A number of questions arise in developing employee training programs. They include:

What are the basic objectives of the training? Are they remedial, or for new skill development?

How will the training meet organizational and employee needs?

What methods should be used? Textbook, lecture, on-the-job, vestibule, simulation? All methods must be evaluated and decided upon.

How can employees be motivated to participate in the training?

How will employees be selected for training programs? By
seniority, merit, or competitive examination? Will they be
stigmatized by not being selected?

If the organization is unionized, how can the union leadership be persuaded to support the training?

Will training take place on employee or organization time?
Will employees be paid fully, partially, or not at all during
training?

What will be the duration of the training program?

Will employees who fail to complete the training successfully still have their old jobs if they were being trained for
new jobs?

How soon will the training be put into practice? Will employees be awarded new jobs as a result of training? Will
promotion be by seniority or merit?

Who will conduct the training? Will only internal personnel
be used, or will outsiders be involved?

What performance measurements will determine progress,
or lack thereof? Will progress be measured by tests, or
instructor's opinion?

Will trainees be permitted to question judgments of their
progress, or lack thereof, that are made by others?

Where will the training take place? Will it be on the prem-
ises, at a local college or university?

What types of follow-up will take place?

These considerations are not all-inclusive, but they do include the most important. None of them can be considered
independently; they are, to a degree, interrelated. That is why
developing a successful program is difficult.

Developing the Program

The first step in developing a program is to define the objectives. The objectives must integrate organization and
employee needs, and should be both general and specific.

Specific objectives might be to: (1) increase production, (2) operate new equipment, (3) improve existing skills, (4) improve cooperation, (5) improve leadership, and (6) reduce accidents.

The approaches and techniques to be used in training must be those that facilitate learning and are affordable. Simulations on electronic equipment may be the best approach, but the cost is often prohibitive. Common air carriers, like United Airlines and Trans World Airlines, have spent a lot of money developing flight simulators, not just because the simulators are effective, but also because the government requires pilot proficiency; having poorly trained pilots flying airplanes carrying hundreds of people would be catastrophic in more ways than one.

Training is not always embraced by employees. Some employees, especially those who have not been in school for many years or did poorly in school, develop real fears of formal training programs. Employees will also ask, ''What do I get out of this?'' Remember, people work for self-serving purposes. If, in their minds, the rewards do not exceed the costs, they are not going to want to participate voluntarily.

Selection for any training program often presents many problems. It is not unusual for training to be looked upon as a form of disciplinary action. ''Why was I selected for the program?'' would be a typical response of someone who thought of training as form of punishment. Training should be looked upon as an opportunity, not as a form of discipline. If seniority is used exclusively to select people for training, the wrong people may be selected. Merit is an elusive concept and merit criteria must be objectively defined and measured. If selection is based on competitive examinations, the tests must meet all of the validity and reliability criteria. Most selection procedures are a combination of seniority and merit. Determining definitions and weighting of factors is no easy task.

In the unionized organization, training programs must receive union support or they usually fail. Unions can be very political and the politics of the situation must be factored into the development of the program. However, political considerations must not influence decisions to the point where programs fail to meet objectives.

Determining on whose time the training will take place is another difficult problem to resolve. Many employees feel that whenever they participate in any organizational training program, it should be on company time and at full pay. They also believe that if it is not on company time, they should be compensated—even at premium time rates. Whether or not we like these attitudes, they must be taken into consideration.

The duration of any training must consider objectives, need, time required to develop high job proficiency, and the trainee's ability to assimilate knowledge that can be put into practice.

Employees are naturally going to be concerned about the risks of participating in any type of training. No one likes to fail. If employees lose the right to go back to their old jobs, or if they should fail in a program that was preparing them for a new job, many will be reluctant to take the risk. However, there are some advantages to taking risk, and the more self-confident employees will do so. If these are the types of people who are desired for the program, maintaining the one-way-street policy will serve to keep out those who are not risk takers.

No organization wants to be in the position of training after the need has materialized. What organizations want is to have trained people available for jobs as the jobs become available. When this is not accomplished, training will be going on while the competition, which trained its employees in advance of need, will be capturing the market. As stated, training must take place before the actual need manifests itself. However, the time between the completion of training and the utilization of skills must be considered. Learned skills that are not applied in a reasonable period of time may diminish rapidly. The number of jobs available for successful trainees can be another problem. The optimal solution is a job for every successful trainee, but this is often not the case. How jobs are awarded is yet another problem. Seniority, age, or grades on exams as criteria for awarding jobs have advantages and disadvantages. The optimal approach is to use the degree of success in completing the training as the primary consideration. Consideration of seniority should be limited. Seniority is best used when two candidates for a job are of equal merit. In this case, seniority should be the determining factor.

Selection of the people who will conduct the training is another decision that must be made. Cost certainly enters into the picture. Outside experts will be expensive, but this can be offset by their higher skill and ability to impart knowledge quickly and accurately. Outsiders may also have more credibility with trainees. Internal personnel are usually more knowledgeable about the organization's environment and needs, but they may lack sophistication in teaching techniques and credibility with trainees.

Performance measurement must be correlated to the type of training and its objectives. Implicit in performance measurement are counseling and feedback to trainees. The objective of performance measurement is to assess performance as a method of constructive feedback. Trainees who meet or exceed expectations must be rewarded, while rehabilitative efforts must be applied to the trainees whose performance is below standard. Trainees must believe that their progress will be measured accurately and fairly. One of the best ways of insuring this is to establish a meaningful procedure for resolving complaints. Nearly all unionized organizations have one, and all nonunion organizations should have some type of complaint-resolution system in operation.

Where the training will take place is an easy decision. Factors considered would be cost, convenience, and quality of facilities. Follow-up is important. Training must be translated into on-the-job performance. Follow-up helps to improve the program and to correct any on-the-job problems that were caused by weaknesses in existing programs.

Applying Learning Theory to Training

Learning can be defined as any relatively permanent change in a person's behavior resulting from reinforced practice. When supervisors see a change in employees' behavior, especially if it takes place after some training, they should interpret this to mean that the employees have learned something. Keep in mind that people are motivated to serve their own interests, and they behave in ways that they are comfortable with and are rewarding to them.

When trainees perceive a benefit from training, they will make themselves receptive to the information associated with the training. Results that reinforce trainees' original behaviors serve to reinforce trainees' desire to continue learning. Reinforcers would include raises, encouragement, praise, recognition, and success through performance.

People vary widely in their ability to accurately assimilate knowledge. In training situations people are continually bombarded with information. If the training takes place too intensely or rapidly, at some point diminishing returns will set in and the trainee will be unable either to retain much of the information or put it into proper relationships. The result is often confusion and frustration for trainees.

As trainees absorb information and interpret it, they should begin to apply the information by practicing. The sooner trainees can apply learning to the job, the sooner they are going to be able to see the application of the training. The application of learning may be done on the job itself in the work environment or in a simulated workplace. Whenever trainees are put into jobs and the learning is incomplete, as shown by inadequate performance, counseling and guidance by the trainer is necessary.

The learning curve

Supervisors must recognize that learning often follows what is known as a learning curve. Various types of training for different people will affect the slopes of learning curves. Usually, when employees are first learning how to do something, the observed performance tends to be slow. It is often difficult to fully comprehend the new learning. As trainees increase their skill and proficiency, performance often improves rapidly, but it is possible over the long run for diminishing returns to set in. This happens when employees become overtrained for jobs or when jobs lose their challenge. Learning curves can be broken down into stages.

At the first stage of learning, the material is all or mostly foreign, and trainees may feel lost and confused. The higher the degree of difficulty in the new material, the higher the probability that barriers to learning will be erected. The communication of knowledge must be geared to trainees' ability to assimilate and translate it into observable and measurable behavior.

The second stage of learning is a rapid growth period as the knowledge communicated gets sorted out and concrete images are developed by trainees. In effect, the trainees are catching on. Catching on can become the main incentive to motivate trainees to continue learning.

At the third stage of learning, a sort of plateau is reached. Additional training does not result in proportional increases in performance. The supervisor and trainees may be deceived into believing that optimum proficiency has been obtained. Two reasons generally account for this plateau. First, trainees are not as strongly motivated to learn as they were in the early phases of training when the successes were larger. Further progress may only come at the expense of considerable effort. Second, trainees need longer periods of time to practice and use additional bits of information they have received.

After a settling process takes place and trainees grow more confident of their understanding and skill, they will enter the fourth stage, the stage of peak proficiency. The fifth stage of learning is the overlearning period achieved by continued repetition, reinforcement, and feedback. Overlearning diminishes the likelihood that trainees will forget if temporarily transferred to other jobs and then returned. The danger in overlearning is that diminishing returns can set in.

Training programs can be well designed and employees can be motivated to participate, but the results can still fall short of expectation. Problems often occur for some of the following reasons:

• People can absorb information only at certain rates. One person's ability may be dramatically different from that of another. The knowledge communicated must be geared to trainees' abilities to absorb and retain.

• Training programs are often started without taking the

time to gain the confidence, enthusiasm, trust, and support of trainees. It is not unusual to see people in training programs who don't know why they were selected, how they were selected, and what changes in behavior are expected as a result of the training.

• Expected rates of progress are often not communicated to trainees. Methods of measuring progress and feedback often do not exist. Perhaps the biggest problem is that trainees are often not properly rewarded for their success in learning. Failure to reinforce through rewards will always cause problems.

• Trainees are not given sufficient time to practice what they have learned. Practice is essential to help make knowledge permanent.

4

Improving communication
with employees, peers,
and superiors

COMMUNICATION is implicit in all aspects of the supervisory role. Every chapter in this book deals in part with communication processes, but this chapter is specifically about communication in order to give an overview of it as a process. Communications, which have many sources and are transmitted in many ways, often end by failing to bring about the results expected or intended. If what causes or affects communication problems can be identified and studied, techniques and approaches designed to correct problems can be developed and implemented.

Human beings are social creatures, and therefore need to communicate and interact with one another. Each of us spends a considerable amount of time during every day of our lives communicating. Of the many problems that confront organizations and their managers, communication nearly always appears at the top, or close to the top of any list. In any formal or informal leadership position, it is necessary for the leader to be able to effectively communicate with followers. Supervisors may be knowledgeable, practical, or popular, but if they are ineffective communicators, they are apt to be unsuccessful.

Effective communication involves the transfer of information with intended meaning in ways that permit those to whom the information is transmitted to receive, interpret, and act upon it in the way intended. In other words, communication is the process of imparting ideas in ways that are understood by others.

Supervisors who fail to communicate effectively eventually lose touch with others. Effective supervisors must be able to sense the temperature and pulse of employees. Sensing is accomplished by communication. Supervisors and their employees function in horizontal and vertical interlocking, or linking-pin, communication roles. (See Figure 1.) Each link represents an organizational unit or group. The pins on each link represent supervisors and employees. The pin at the apex of each link represents the supervisor. In most organizations, people in one group are linked by formal and informal relationships with people in other groups. The more formal and informal interaction that takes place, the more linking arrangements exist. The type of communication and the people involved in the processes define linking-pin arrangements. Linking-pin communication structures are dynamic because they continually change as formal and informal relationships change.

Supervisors, in linking-pin communication roles, have a

Figure 1. Linking pin communication system.

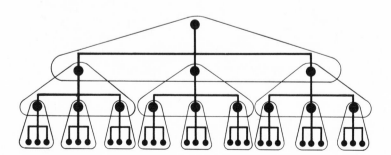

From *New Patterns of Management* by Rensis Likert. Copyright © 1961, McGraw-Hill Book Company. Used with permission.

considerable amount of information moving through them; from higher levels of the organization down, from employees up, and horizontally through peer interaction. Most supervisors make a sincere effort to communicate with their employees, peers, and superiors. They do so because they recognize that without the continuous movement of information, resultant problems will impede attaining objectives. However, supervisors often become frustrated because communication processes do not work in practice as smoothly as they do in theory. To be effective communicators, supervisors must be effective listeners. Real communication occurs when the receivers of communications act, or react, in the ways expected, or desired, by the message sender. Real communication means that in formulating communications, supervisors are sensitive to the needs and viewpoints of others. They also objectively consider the receiver's point of view when listening to them.

If any communication is to achieve its objective, it must be understood. Everyone has had moments of frustration when communicating with others. It is very frustrating to learn that a communication has been partially or totally misunderstood after it was thought to have been communicated in as clear and straightforward a manner as possible.

Why do misunderstandings or misinterpretations occur in communicating? Although communication is a complicated process, the facets of the process can be shown by a basic illustration. As Figure 2 shows, an idea is originated with the

Figure 2

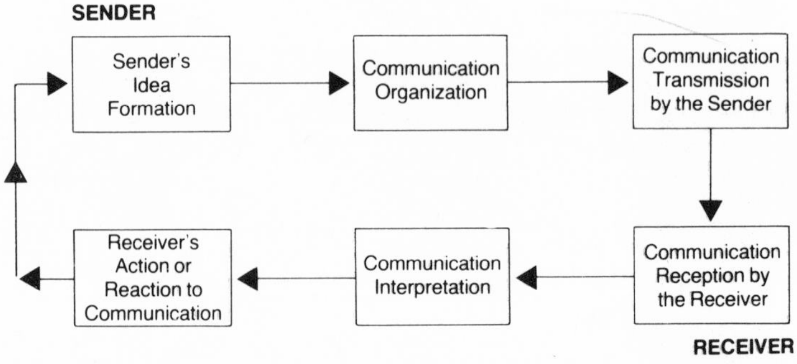

desire to communicate it to others. The originator of the idea encodes it into some communicable form, oral or written, and communicates through symbols, sounds, gestures, expressions, writing, or visual displays, directly or indirectly to the intended recipient. By direct or indirect means, the recipient receives the communication, decodes it, and acts or reacts to it. The process of action or reaction as communicated back to the sender is feedback. From feedback, the sender is able to assess whether or not the communication has been received, interpreted, and acted upon as expected or desired.

Barriers to Effective Communication

There are numerous reasons why people fail to communicate effectively. It would be impossible in one chapter to provide even nominal discussion of all of the types of barriers; however, the major sources of communication problems are identified and discussed in this section. Supervisors should consider to what extent the barriers discussed are impeding communication with people in their organization and units.

Sentiments

In relations with others, each person views the world with biases, prejudices, values, feelings, attitudes, experiences, and beliefs—in a word, sentiments. Sentiments act as filters. Each person views and interprets the world through filters; through these filters, one can interpret anything in any way. For example, suppose one were to look at a green chalkboard, often referred to as a blackboard, and conclude that the board was black, not green. After all, if it were green, wouldn't it be called a greenboard? Once you have arranged your filters to interpret green to be black, it would be difficult to convince you otherwise.

Figure 3 illustrates how communication between two people can be distorted through sentiments, or filters. Each circle represents a filter. The number of filters through which communications are transmitted or received can be selectively var-

Figure 3

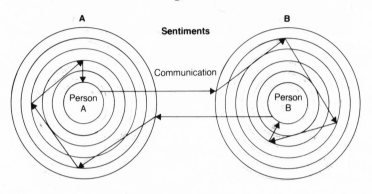

ied by senders or receivers. In addition, the strength of any filter can change. For example, a feeling about someone, whether it is good or bad, can change in an instant, or over time.

Language

In communication we rely heavily upon the use of language. Language may be spoken, unspoken, or written. This section will pertain to spoken and written language. Even when people speak the same language, the meaning of words can vary widely. For example, government rules, regulations, and procedures, although employing the English language, are usually written in such a way as to totally confuse most readers. Figure 4 is an example of government's debased use of language.

Advertisements skillfully use language to create certain images or impressions that may be accurate, partially accurate, or totally inaccurate in relation to the product or service being promoted. The legal and medical professions are notorious for using the English language in ways that, unless a person has had training in those areas, make it difficult to understand their communications. Why the medical, and particularly the legal professions, go to such great lengths to abuse the English language could generate some interesting discussions.

Figure 4

MAKING IT PERFECTLY CLEAR

The Federal Register's
horrible example of bureaucratese:

"We respectfully petition, request, and entreat that due and adequate provision be made, this day and the date hereinafter subscribed, for the satisfying of these petitioners' nutritional requirements and for the organizing of such methods of allocation and distribution as may be deemed necessary and proper to assure the reception by and for said petitioners of such quantities of baked cereal products as shall, in the judgment of the aforesaid petitioners, constitute a sufficient supply thereof."

—*Federal government English*

Translation: "Give us this day our daily bread."

—*King James English*

Reprinted from the May 9, 1977, issue of *Business Week* by special permission.

We learn to use language early in life. As we age, our skill in using language changes. Education, home and peer influences, exposure, experience, and application all affect our use of language. Language is one way by which people identify and relate to one another. Cultural, social, educational, age, ethnic, political, religious, professional, and racial groups all use language in particular ways to identify who is in and who is out of the group. The language of the ghetto is strikingly different from the language of the middle class. For example, the word "horse" to some people means the drug heroin, while to others it is a four-legged animal. The more any group modifies the meaning of language, the more they can use language to differentiate themselves. Why groups choose to distinguish themselves from others has been the subject of considerable research.

Organizations are usually composed of people who differ considerably in age, education, culture, religious views, skills, and professions. There is a distinct tendency for various levels and groups within organizations to develop a language that is unique and germane to itself. That personnel, marketing, engineering, production, legal, administrative, and other groups develop their unique definitions and uses of language is a major source of organizational communication problems.

Figure 5 illustrates a different view of an organizational communication structure. Members of each group, by their use of the language which is germane to the profession or group, will experience difficulty communicating with members of other groups. Misinterpretations and misunderstandings will cause friction between groups who do not speak the same language. Groups that have similar values and language will be inclined to interact with one another rather than with people they do not understand, or who do not understand them.

However, the requirements of roles and jobs often require that people or groups interact. The result is often friction, which causes sparks of conflict. To avoid the heat of conflict, groups often keep communication with those outside the group

Figure 5. Communication conflict.

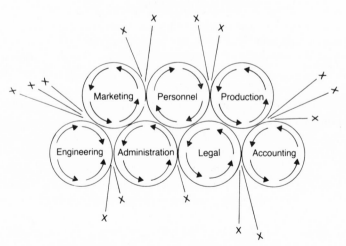

to the necessary minimum. This, of course, usually adversely affects cooperation and organization performance.

The one way to resolve communication conflict is to simplify the use of language throughout the organization and compel people to work together toward solving common problems or achieving common goals. Mutual dependency can go a long way toward reducing problems of communication or other forms of conflict. What cannot continue to occur is for groups who do not communicate to be allowed to continue the practice. The same can be said for similar types of communication problems within any group that is composed of people who are widely different from one another.

Prejudice and bias

Everyone has biases or prejudices. People tend to acquire most of their prejudices before adulthood. Throughout their lives people modify, drop, or reinforce biases and prejudices. They develop stereotyped pictures and definitions of others based on one or a combination of factors. For example, teenager, Catholic, Baptist, Jew, engineer, Black, Irishman, Italian, senior citizen, and accountant are words that communicate an image or an idea. When people classify and stereotype others, they tend to apply their feelings and beliefs to all people who fall within the classification. Supervisors must understand the reasons underlying these prejudices and work toward overcoming or controlling them. Prejudices or biases are not easily concealed, and many people have developed a sensitivity toward identifying prejudice in others. Prejudices distort the encoding, transmission, receiving, interpreting, acting on, or reacting to information.

In addition to general prejudices or biases, people have situational prejudices or biases. A man may not have a general prejudice toward women, but when a woman is in a position outside of what is perceived to be her normal role, prejudice may arise. This type of prejudice is sometimes exhibited toward women who are in management. The same could be said of men who keep the home, cook, and shop for groceries. Again, the prejudice is not toward men in general. It is toward them when they function in what is considered by some to be a woman's role. As everyone knows, we live in a changing world and must be prepared to adapt to change. In other words, prejudices often outlive their validity.

Position, role, and importance in an organization

Organizations are environments of inequality. Authority, influence, title, function, position, compensation, and status are just a few of the bases by which people are differentiated. Differences among people in organizations become apparent when communication takes place. The differences in education, background, title, uniform, and even office decor often cause anxiety and apprehension in upward communication. It is not unusual for supervisors to feel some anxiety when they discuss a concern or idea with the company president, especially if it is discussed in the president's office. These unavoidable inequalities cause problems.

Differences in values are evident in upward, and particularly downward, communication. For example, managers often think of change as a way to increase productivity, market penetration, revenue, and profits. Workers often interpret change to mean increased job responsibilities, changes in social position, security, and wages. While profits and wages are directly related, the average worker often does not fully understand this fundamental relationship. Whether communication is upward or downward, receivers interpret it through their filters. Receivers' sentiments will cause selective filtration of communication. A key factor in minimizing the filtration problem is to communicate in terms of receivers' values and in language they understand.

Accurate upward communication is also difficult to achieve because people will act, or react, in light of their perceptions of the information's possible effect upon their power and prestige. Also, some people are not very receptive to hearing bad news. Rather than communicate bad news, it is often safer to communicate what the boss wants to hear, or even nothing at all. Still another reason for supervisors' reluctance to communicate bad news to *their* supervisors is the fear that it will reflect unfavorably upon their own proficiency as managers.

Time

Timing of communication is very important. Anyone who has participated in negotiations or other sensitive actions has seen the use of timing. When communication is timed improperly, the result is often not what was expected or intended. For example, suppose you want to ask your boss for a raise. After some deliberation, you decide that this is the day. You arrive at work, and when you enter your boss's office he proceeds to inform you about various errors, losses, and other negative conditions related to your performance. You listen to his remarks and then, in accordance with your decision, you ask him for a raise. What are your chances of getting the raise? Not too good! Why? Your timing was off. His frame of mind was such that a request for a raise would not be favorably received.

Sometimes delaying the sending of information is desirable. However, most often communications need to move rapidly so they can be received, analyzed, and acted upon. In business competition, or warfare, failure to receive accurate information in a timely manner usually results in delayed and often poor decisions. The result of continued delays in the communication of information is failure.

Space

People are territorially conscious creatures. The use of space is very important in communication. Generally, people of higher status demand more space, or what can be called territorial circles. Animals often urinate or defecate to define their territory. People use other means. In organizations, office space, desk size, seating arrangements, and decor all reflect one's position and hence the amount of space allowed. Depending upon the type of information, structure, and parties to the communication, space requirements can expand, contract, or remain the same.

People's space requirements are not always clearly defined. However, once the territorial circle is trespassed, reaction will occur. Reaction may be offensive or defensive. To illustrate the use of space in communication, try asking your boss for a raise from a distance of about one foot from his face. You certainly will have infringed upon his territory. Your chances of getting a favorable decision are reduced. However, in a different situation, and with a different person, communication in close proximity may be desirable. For example, two lovers may merge their respective territories to facilitate intimate communication.

This has been only a partial discussion of the barriers to effective communication. Supervisors must be sensitive to barriers and work toward overcoming them if they are to be effective. Recognition of a barrier is half the solution toward controlling or removing it. Following are additional barriers that may be encountered in communication. These are of three classes: general, upward, and downward.

General barriers:
    Failure to understand personal motives
    Showing unconcern or not giving feedback
    Feelings of self-righteousness
    Perceived superiority or inferiority
    Protection of one's prestige
    Improper role playing
    Noise, distraction, lack of privacy
    Hidden agenda or messages
    Lack of clarity in intent and meaning
    Failure to express conviction
    Poor listening habits
    Telling half truths
Upward barriers:
    Intimidating employees
    Not finding time to listen
    Lack of concern
    Weak leadership
    Being distrusted
    Talking down to employees
Downward barriers:
    Suspicion, fear, mistrust
    Lack of confidence
    Tendency to prejudge
    Value system and language differences

Understanding Communication Channels

Communication is a complex process, and easy solutions to an organization's communication problems are rare. Supervisors, in their relationships with others, must carefully examine all facets of the communication process. These include the environment, the situation, and the persons involved in the underlying causes of problems. Most communication problems in organizations stem from problems in relationships. Problem-solving approaches such as writing more effectively or learning how to give a speech, while useful, rarely get to the underlying causes. Therefore, they often do not bring about the problem-solving results expected.

In organizations, communications generally move through two identifiable channels. One is the formal channel, or network, and the other the informal channel, commonly known as the grapevine.

Formal channels, or networks

Formal communication channels are established by formal relationships, job descriptions, task assignments, methods, practices, technology, laws, procedures, rules, and regulations. These channels are easily identified by the formal lines of authority and responsibility—organization charts, organizational policy manuals, and standard operating procedures.

In most organizations, formal communication processes and channels tend to become set in concrete. Since power and status are associated with initiating, distributing, and receiving communications, it is easy to understand why so much emotion surrounds organization information systems. It is also easy to understand why there is often great reluctance to change established flows. Changes in information flows usually cause changes in power and relationships. Understandably, those who will lose power or status are going to be reluctant to accept, let alone initiate, change.

When they feel it is necessary, supervisors, as well as others, have a responsibility to question the validity and reliability of information communicated through established channels, or networks. Movement of information must facilitate the accomplishment of objectives. As objectives, or the approaches to achieving the objectives change, the systems that generate and distribute information must also change. Unnecessary and improper movement of information wastes time, energy, talent, and money.

Notable examples of where these problems exist are government and business organizations where meaningful competition does not exist. Unnecessary communications often emanate from supportive, or so-called staff personnel. In general, the product of staff efforts is paperwork in the form of procedures, processes, directives, and methods. To justify their existence, staff must produce paperwork and other forms of communications. In fact, in some organizations people may generate unnecessary information to build their prestige and influence. Such practices are commonly referred to as empire building. People who engage in these practices go to great lengths to demonstrate the need for and importance of the information they generate, clear, control, or distribute.

Some of the questions that must always be asked when analyzing communications and the channels through which they move are:

To what degree is this information necessary for facilitating the accomplishment of objectives?

What are the true costs of generating and distributing this information?

Who was involved in the generation of the information? Who is involved in its distribution? What are their motives or involvement?

Is it necessary for the people who are currently involved to remain involved in the generation, distribution, or receiving functions?

If this information is necessary, can the costs of generating and redistributing it be reduced? How much can it be reduced?

How valid and reliable is the information?

It must be remembered that when changing any facet of a communication process, a great deal of organization politics is involved. Needless to say, considerable skill is required to change a system without generating an avalanche of problems. Most supervisors lack the authority to change formal organization communication channels. However, they can point out to others who have authority the reasons why change needs to take place. This may involve personal risk, but effective supervisors are risk takers.

Supervisors, in using formal channels of communication, tend to place heaviest emphasis on the downward flow of information when communicating with employees. Downward communication helps to link the different levels of the organization together. Unfortunately, not enough emphasis is placed on developing good channels of upward communication. Effective upward communication starts at the bottom of the organization and moves through each level all the way to the top. It is incumbent upon all levels of supervision to create an environment where employees feel free to communicate feelings and concerns, as well as accomplishments and activities, to supervisors. The feedback that takes place through upward communication is necessary for supervisors to determine if what has been transmitted to employees has been received, properly understood, and will be complied with to the degree expected.

In general, downward communication serves to initiate the feedback process. The content of downward communication is mostly of an informative or directive nature. The resultant upward communication tends to be more of a questioning and reporting nature, including suggestions, concerns, and complaints or grievances. Compared to the roars generated by downward communication, upward communication tends to be in whispers. In creating the proper environment for accurate upward communication, supervisors must show that they want the straight facts about employees' feelings and concerns. It is very difficult in any organization to establish and maintain a climate that is free of risk in upward communication. When we speak of upward communication, we are again dealing with different levels of power and status in the organization. Even under the best conditions, it may be difficult for employees to be totally candid with the people who determine whether they retain their jobs, get a raise, or assign them work.

Supervisors must remember that if employees do not have channels within the organization through which they can communicate their feelings and concerns, these feelings, concerns, and the like will find other outlets within or outside of the organization. The results are usually undesirable. When negative feelings are expressed within the community through family, friends, and social interaction, the organization's image suffers. Today, as never before, good employees are hard to find. No organization, because it has a bad image, wants to be the employer of last resort. In addition, society allows organizations the privilege of serving. When society perceives that the disadvantages of an organization's operational behavior exceed the benefits, society, through the market or government regulation, will take what it believes to be the proper corrective action.

When upward communication does not work and employees' emotions are expressed in many different ways and directions within the organization, the results are often costly problems. When employees' feelings are not expressed at all, they will build to a critical level, and may result in some type of explosive emotional reaction, such as sabotage, walkouts, lawsuits, civil actions, and unionization attempts. The key to avoiding these types of problems is to develop an operational climate with appropriate channels through which frustrations, concerns, and anxieties can be constructively expressed and meaningful results obtained.

In addition to downward and upward communication, there are horizontal channels of communication. The horizontal channels may also be multidirectional, because they are affected by the formal organization's structure and the dynamics of the informal structure. The flow of lateral information in the organization is essential because of the high degree of interrelatedness and interdependency of work in modern organizations.

Informal channels, or grapevines

Many supervisors fear grapevines and try to eliminate them. Elimination of informal communication systems is not only undesirable, it is an absolute impossibility. If one channel is destroyed, another will be immediately established. This occurs because of the nature of the interrelationships of people. Effective supervisors learn to cultivate grapevines carefully and use them in ways that benefit the organization, employees, and themselves.

Supervisors should develop an ear for listening to grapevine communications. It helps give insight into what employees are thinking. Information that moves through grapevines tends to be partially correct. Distortions occur because of private interpretations and rumors. While grapevines are prone to distortion, they have the advantage of moving information quickly. They go around or cut across formal organizational lines.

Because of unstable social relationships, grapevines have no explicitly defined pattern or duration. Participation in grapevines varies according to the formal structure, the informal social structure, people who have access to the information, people who are affected by the information, and other variables. It is recognized that the people who tend to be very active in grapevine communication are those who either have, or are aspiring to, social position or popularity.

One of the dangers in grapevine systems is the degree of distortion that takes place; from distortions, rumors often arise. Supervisors can minimize distortion problems by following a few simple rules. First, establish a relationship of trust and confidence with employees. Employees must see supervisors as people who will give straight answers to questions, or reasons why answers cannot be given. Second, never make the mistake of lying to employees. If a supervisor ever lies to employees, it is best to take corrective action by confessing to the lie and then being honest with them in the future. An admitted mistake is more likely to be forgiven. A covered-up mistake that is later uncovered is usually not forgiven. Third, supervisors should anticipate what types of information will cause concern among employees. By explaining the meaning of certain changes to employees, before distorted meanings are generated, problems can be minimized. When employees do not have accurate information as to the meaning of changes, they will develop their own. Grapevines tend to become most active during periods when employees are experiencing high degrees of apprehension, anxiety, frustration, tension, or insecurity brought about by actual or expected changes within the organization.

In any organization, there are people who attempt to increase their influence, or information power. They often attempt to do this at the expense of the authority, prestige, and influence of supervisors. Some employees find it to their advantage to cultivate or embellish rumors, especially when in doing so they increase their prestige with their peers. This type of situation can readily result in a power confrontation between the employees and supervisors. Supervisors who have established relationships of trust and confidence with employees, and especially the informal group leaders, will be able to easily deal with the employees who are trying to gain politically at their expense. In these situations, all the supervisor has to do is tell the employees who trust him what they have heard is not correct, and that the person who has told them this information has distorted the facts, or lied, whichever is the case. The solution to the problem has been put into motion. Employees will discredit an unpopular rumor starter. On the other hand, the effectiveness of a supervisor who is not held in high regard by employees is limited in trying to discredit rumors and rumor starters. In some instances, mistrusted supervisors who attempt to discredit a rumor may find their efforts turned against them by the rumor starters. Therefore, it is obvious that an effective supervisor must have the trust and confidence of a majority of the group, and especially the informal group leaders.

Supervisors can manage the grapevine system in another way. They can communicate to employees through the grapevine information that they do not wish to communicate formally. For example, a supervisor might recognize that formal discipline of an employee would generate the wrong results. He could use the informal communication system to inform the employee that his performance is not up to expectations and that if change does not occur, formal action will be taken. Peers often have more latitude in saying things to one another than supervisors have with employees.

Effective Communication with Others

Supervisors, as influencers of people's behavior, must be able to sell ideas to others. It is easy to assert authority and direct that something be done; it is always more difficult to persuade someone to do something voluntarily. Supervisors often recognize the need for change long before the need is recognized by higher management. However, supervisors often lack the authority to bring about change. Because upward communication involves risk taking, many supervisors withdraw into their position descriptions and avoid the risk of telling their supervisors that change is needed. This is especially true when the boss does not want to hear certain things, or has rejected previous suggestions. To a lesser degree, the same can be said in communication with employees and peers. When employees have the right to appeal a decision or are represented by a strong union, supervisors sometimes find it more convenient to do nothing, rather than to take a risk. Apathy in management is dangerous.

Effective supervisors learn to package or repackage their ideas and persevere in attempting to influence their supervisors and others. In effect, they are not easily rebuffed. Some use the bull in the china shop approach, while others avoid breaking the china. How is it that some supervisors continually fail to sell their ideas, while others, who often sell the same ideas, succeed? Those who succeed usually apply a few recognized guidelines to their communications.

Communications are always more effective when they are receiver oriented. When information relates to people's values, they will be more inclined to listen. For example, management's values tend to revolve around profits, growth, and productivity. Employees' values tend to revolve around wages, security, and social relationships with peers. A message to employees about change that emphasizes the need to change for reasons of profits and production will not be so effective as the same message emphasizing the need for change in order to maintain wages and job security.

When supervisors are not trusted, or others lack confidence in them, it will affect communications. Salespeople learn to quickly gain the trust and confidence of those whom they want to influence in order to increase their chances of making a sale. Trust and confidence are difficult to maintain. Employees tend to be wary when interacting with their supervisors. In the long run, people will be judged by what they do rather than by what they say. It is better to say nothing than to lie about, or distort, information.

Effective communicators learn to plan and organize their communications before they actually communicate. Some people are inclined to suffer from verbal diarrhea. Again, it may be better to say nothing than to communicate for the sake of filling time gaps or space on a piece of paper. Advertisers long ago learned how to plan and organize their communications. At today's prices for television and radio time and print space, communications that are poorly planned and organized waste a lot of money.

Vocabulary and delivery

Since most communication in organizations requires the use of written and spoken language, the choice of words is important. The English language, in particular, is very complex, with words often having multiple meanings. In addition, different words mean the same thing. Because of their backgrounds, experiences, values, and the like, people attach different meanings to words. S. I. Hayakawa, the U.S. Senator from California, and Victor Borge, the famous entertainer, from different perspectives, have informed and amused us with their discussions of the use and misuse of language.

Because language in communications must be receiver oriented, using words that people do not understand will usually cause receivers to be turned off. Most people are reluctant to use a dictionary or ask for clarification. Nobody likes to display ignorance. This is true throughout all levels of organizations. On the opposite side of the coin is the use of language that is too simple. This often causes receivers to perceive that the communications are condescending, and they resent being spoken down to. Again, it asserts the inequalities among people. The key is to use plain English, although some words may be used that are not in the everyday language of receivers. It is preferable to communicate slightly above receivers instead of slightly below them.

In communication where the speaker is observed, body language is important. Appearance, posture, eye contact, facial expressions, arm waving, finger pointing, foot stomping, and the like can either enhance or detract from communication. Communicators who are successful influencers know how to put their whole personality into communication. Their body movements and speech complement one another. One visit to a discotheque will demonstrate the effective use of body language by both men and women. As part of effective oral communication, vocal qualities are important. Pitch, tone, articulation, volume, and rate of speech all influence spoken messages. Speaking too softly or too loudly may be irritating and distracting to receivers.

Timing

Effective communicators develop a sense of timing. Knowing when to communicate a message is just as important as knowing how to communicate it. When a message is communicated, feedback will occur if it was received. Feedback is essential, and is obtained only when the receiver is a good listener. Remember, what is communicated must lead to action. People must react to communications.

Two techniques for obtaining and assessing feedback are: First, ask the person to whom the communication was directed to repeat the message and what it means to him. If the listener can repeat the message with the proper interpretation, it is safe to conclude that it was understood. Understanding does not mean that the expected or desired action will occur. Second, judge the listener's behavior after the message was received. Body movements, facial expressions, changes in posture, and eye movements all provide nonverbal feedback to message senders. This form of feedback can only be observed in face-to-face communication.

Good listening habits can be developed by following a few simple guidelines:

- Some speakers are not very articulate and therefore have difficulty expressing their thoughts and feelings. Others are long winded and take what seems to be forever to make their point. Good listeners learn to be patient. Impatient listeners may motivate speakers to stop communicating.
- It is difficult to keep listening to a message while disagreeing with its content. Even though disagreement exists, good listeners continue to listen so they can properly assess the complete message and react to it. Prejudgment, or impulsive judgment, is detrimental to good listening.
- Some speakers display annoying mannerisms or project a negative image. Good listeners do not let prejudice or bias affect their receiving and interpreting communications.
- When people do not understand the message being communicated, they usually stop listening rather than ask for clarification. A good listener asks for clarification of what is not understood.
- Some people would rather talk than listen. A good listener waits until the message sender is finished before replying.

What Should Be Communicated to Employees

Supervisors, by virtue of their roles as leaders, are often privy to more information about the organization than employees. Sometimes information is of a sensitive or confidential nature. Employees, to varying degrees, are curious about the effect decisions made by others will have on them. It is important for employees to feel a sense of belonging to the organization. When they can identify in a positive way with their jobs, coworkers, management, and the organization's products or services, fewer problems are apt to occur.

No organization can be completely open with its employees about all its operations. Leaks of confidential or sensitive, or even general information can have adverse consequences for employees, management, the organization, and others. What information should be communicated by supervisors and others to employees? Following are examples of information that employees usually need or want to know:

- The history of the organization, its products or services, and how the products or services are developed and marketed. Most employees know little of what their organization does and how it operates.
- Organizational policies and procedures that affect them.
- Major organizational plans for change and how employees will be affected. More than anything else that employees want to know, such information must be properly timed. Too much information too soon could be just as disastrous as too little too late.
- The ways in which employees' jobs fit into the organization's operations. It is important to show employees that their jobs are important to the organization.
- How the organization's system of promotion and other rewards function.
- How the organization's rules, regulations, and disciplinary system function.
- How employees can get a hearing for their complaints or grievances.
- The organization's future in terms of its short- and long-range objectives. The prospects for steady employment and opportunities for advancement.
- The organization's general financial condition. The disclosure of profits, for example, must be tempered, because many employees cannot properly evaluate the concepts of return on investment or the need to invest money in new equipment to maintain competitive advantage.
- Information about layoffs, if they should become necessary. The reasons for layoffs as well as their possible duration should be communicated.

This list is not all inclusive by any means, but it can be helpful to supervisors in planning and organizing communications with employees. Supervisors should develop their own lists of what they think employees should know.

5

Understanding leadership and developing an effective leadership style

WHENEVER people voluntarily, or involuntarily, work together toward the accomplishment of common objectives, an organization comes into existence. In formal or informal organizations, some person or group will emerge to direct and coordinate the activities of others for the purpose of accomplishing objectives or goals. Leadership in organizations has been observed throughout recorded history, and existed in prehistoric times. There are many ways by which leaders are chosen or emerge, and there are many reasons why some people want to lead.

If leadership is absent or ineffective in an organization, members will behave in ways that cause problems which, if not resolved, will lead to eventual chaos. When leadership is present and effective, the activities of others are defined and carried out so that objectives are achieved with a minimum of problems. Leadership positions, or roles, exist in organizations because they are necessary. People who lead may acquire their positions and roles by violent or nonviolent seizure, election, creating them, or by some system of formal or informal succession. In the long run, leaders remain effective only if their followers are willing to cooperate. Cooperation may be achieved by force, or it may come about voluntarily. It is usually preferable to secure cooperation by voluntary rather than forceful means.

In free societies, membership in organizations, whether they are religious, commercial, governmental, or military, is usually voluntary. When membership is voluntary, leaders must influence people to want to stay and cooperate instead of psychologically or physically withdraw or rebel. When membership is involuntary and penalties for not cooperating are high, leaders can exploit members for personal benefit. They can continue to exploit others for as long as they have sufficient power to quell thoughts or actions of resistance.

As discussed in earlier chapters, people join organizations to satisfy needs. Organizations recruit, hire, and retain people to satisfy needs. Leaders have the responsibility of maintaining a delicate balance between satisfying the needs of organizations, the needs of members, and their own needs.

Whether or not leadership is effective involves the complex interrelationships of leaders, followers, internal and external environments, and many other circumstances and conditions. Some of these factors are laws, the state of the economy, the organization's position in the industry, and its financial condition, philosophy, traditions, practices, customers, technology, capitalization, size, and structure.

Management literature contains a rich and diverse assortment of information about every conceivable aspect of leadership. There is so much fragmented information that only a portion of it could be assimilated in a reasonable amount of time. The literature is so diverse that the more one reads the more confused one gets. In recent years, researchers have shown a particularly strong interest in studying the effects of leadership approaches, or styles. It appears that every time a researcher communicates the results of a new study, new terms and phrases are presented. Different names for what are essentially the same approaches or methods add to the confusion about leadership. In addition, many researchers study leadership in organizations on a comparatively small scale and then commit the error of making grandiose findings and conclusions.

The author will not elaborate upon the specific research findings of notable researchers like Simon, Likert, McGregor, Fiedler, Herzberg, Blake and Mouton, Argyris, Whyte, Lewin, and countless others who have made meaningful contributions. Instead, the author will attempt to discuss leadership from broader perspectives with the objective of helping supervisors to understand leadership and to use this knowledge to assess their own effectiveness. Supervisors, by objectively assessing the results of their leadership styles, can then determine if change is required to increase effectiveness.

Broadly generalized, leadership styles range from highly directive, or authoritarian, to highly nondirective, or participative. An example of an authoritarian style would be a supervisor's ordering an employee to do something without giving the employee any right or opportunity to question the order. An example of a participative approach would be a supervisor's discussing various courses of action with employees and allowing them to participate in making a decision.

Many writers have tried to convince managers at all levels that a business organization can be managed in a democratic manner where everyone has an equal voice in decisions. In nearly all formal organizations, and especially business organizations, this does not and could not work for any length of time. Even in the United States Senate and House of Representatives, where the members are theoretically equal, this condition does not exist. Some senators and representatives are far more powerful than others. Therefore, they are not all equal.

Most organizations are smaller, or narrower, at the top than at the base. Figure 6 depicts one organization with many levels and one with few levels. While the levels vary in shape and number, they are all smaller at the top than they are at the base. Power and responsibility vary considerably between and among the various levels of any organization. In effect, not all people are equal.

Figure 6

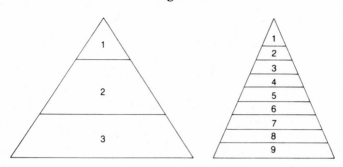

Leaders as Discriminators

Most organizations today experience fundamental problems in exercising their authority because many people believe that everyone should have the same rights, privileges, authorities, and compensation as everyone else. This general belief is known as egalitarianism, and it is incompatible with a healthy capitalistic system. In terms of economic and political philosophy, it is socialism. People may profess that everyone should be treated the same, but in reality they want to be treated as individuals. To prove the point, try this simple experiment. Hire two people and assign them to different tasks. Put one in a very strenuous, demanding assignment and the other one in an easy one. At the end of a specific time period, pay both people the same wages. What will the reaction be? Obviously, the person who performed the more demanding activity will perceive that he has been discriminated against and has been taken advantage of.

If you are still not convinced, consider this. You have just been hired as the general manager of a large organization with a salary of $100,000. Are you happy? Of course. One day you find out that a number of the laborers that were recently hired were hired at a starting salary of $150,000. Now how do you feel about your responsibilities and rewards versus those of the laborers? Not so good. Readers should look around and see the many ways in which people try to differentiate themselves from one another.

Inherently, people do not want to be treated the same as others; they want to be treated fairly and according to merit. The bases upon which people are treated differently and the ways in which they are differentiated from one another have concerned people from the beginning of time. Since people want to be treated differently, managers at all levels must discriminate; discrimination is implicit in the concept of leadership. Failure to discriminate creates instant mediocrity; those who deserve more are inadequately rewarded and those who deserve less are overrewarded. The challenge to all leaders is to discriminate on bases that are legitimate, ethical, and moral and to do it in ways that others perceive as being fair. Only when people perceive that the advantages of everyone's being treated the same are greater than the disadvantages will they opt for the same treatment for all. As discussed in Chapter 2, supervisors must continually find ways to treat people differently and do it in ways that are fair. Fairness is an elusive concept; it will be discussed at length in Chapter 6.

Evolution of Leadership Approaches, or Styles

If we examine the leadership approaches, or styles, practiced by managers in free societies over the last 100 to 150 years, a gradual overall shift in approaches can be observed. Keep in mind that this is a generalization to which there are many exceptions. The approaches or styles have shifted from highly directive, or authoritarian, to more nondirective, or participative, a style that has been mentioned a number of times in this chapter. There appears to be considerable misunderstanding about what participative management is, or is not. It does not mean that supervisors and employees have equal voices in decision making, as some are inclined to believe. In a participatively managed group, employees have meaningful input to the decision-making process, but the final decision rests with the supervisor. The supervisor retains veto power over the recommendations of employees because the supervisor is the person who has the final responsibility for the accomplishment of objectives. To use this approach effectively, supervisors must be willing to listen to and consider employees' input into decision making.

Styles of leadership, in general, have shifted over the years for a number of reasons. Many people in leadership positions have not accepted the idea that today they cannot lead people in the same ways they did in the past. Indeed, most leaders have sort of backed into less authoritarian approaches to managing. Leadership involves the exercise of power, which many people enjoy. The right and ability to exercise power is one of the attractions of leadership positions. This does not mean that all leaders are power hungry and eager to dominate others. It does mean that a lot of satisfaction can be derived from exercising power, especially if it is used to benefit rather than hurt.

In recent years a considerable amount of research and resultant literature have attempted to convince people that nondirective, or participative, styles are the best for all concerned. The facts are that this view is often incorrect. Many things influence the effectiveness or ineffectiveness of leaders and the styles they develop and apply. The gradual shift in applied leadership styles has been caused by the interrelationships of many factors, events, circumstances, and conditions. Broadly speaking, leadership styles have shifted from highly to less directive because of:

Changing social values, for example, egalitarianism.
Legislation protecting workers' rights (civil rights legislation, labor-management relations legislation at all levels of government, work environment and fair employment practices legislation).
Supply and demand in the labor market.
Competition—domestic and foreign.
Declining profit margins.
Unions and their countervailing power.
Higher levels of formal education of workers.
Higher levels of formal education of management.
Increasing costs due to scarcity, higher taxes, and other factors.

It appears that for the foreseeable future, these factors will continue to exert influences upon the leadership styles practiced by all levels of management in organizations.

Changing Attitudes in the Workplace

It is common knowledge that workers today have values and attitudes different from those of workers of a generation ago. Supervisors cannot live in the past, or long for the past when workers were easier to manage. They must recognize what exists and adjust to it. When employees' values are considerably different from those of supervisors, there is going to be conflict. In the short run, supervisors must force their decisions on employees, accept the increased costs of control, compromise and adapt within limits, or capitulate, and, in effect, abandon their role and responsibilities. The long-run solution to employee attitude problems is to educate employees to understand that they can satisfy their needs by cooperating to accomplish organizational goals. It is only a healthy capitalistic system that is able to provide jobs, pay income taxes, and support social programs.

Many employees need to understand that in organizations they cannot always "do their thing." Privileges or freedoms are earned by demonstrating responsible behavior. This process of education, or reeducation, is not an easy task, because many employees, particularly in their formative years, have been educated to believe that business is evil, profits is a dirty word, and capitalism exploits people. Many supervisors would be surprised to learn that the majority of younger workers (those under 25 years of age) have little, if any, real understanding of capitalism in spite of their years of schooling.

Government acts and reacts according to input from society. A democratic government, if it is to survive, must remain popular. To remain popular it must be responsive to society's needs. Society's input into government decision making is often contradictory. One group pushes for one thing and another pushes for the opposite. Because a large portion of society has, sometimes for valid reasons, become suspicious of organizations, in particular businesses, government has enacted and vigorously applied a plethora of laws, regulations, procedures, directives, and rules affecting organizations' functioning. Many of these laws have increased the costs of doing business, restricted decision making, and created artificial demands for employees with special training, such as personnel specialists, attorneys, and accountants. Complying with federal, state, and local laws has been so frustrating and confusing for all levels of management that they sometimes lose sight of the reasons for the organization's existence. Employees have also developed a certain sophistication in calling upon the administrators of the law for protection or justice.

Supervisors must understand the reasons why these laws were enacted and become knowledgeable in how they affect their role as leaders. Supervisors will not be supported by anyone when they operate outside the law. Regrettably, the government's penchant for enacting new laws and its diligence in applying existing ones have not begun to diminish.

For many reasons, we have seen wide variance in the supply and demand factors in the labor market. Technology, population shifts, nonadaptive educational systems, lack of manpower planning, unions, changes in the law, and changing consumer preferences are some of the factors affecting the supply and demand for labor. When certain skilled workers or professionals are in short supply, for example, certain types of engineers, tool and die makers, plumbers, accountants, electricians, or physicians, what is known as a seller's market is created. The people who possess the skills which are in short supply and for which there is high demand have their choice of employers. If they become dissatisfied, because of the way they are treated, they can, and often do, quickly change employers. Loyalty to organizations is a thing of the past. Supervisors must be sensitive to this condition in directing all employees, particularly employees whose skills are in short supply.

Declining profit margins, inflation, rising costs, competition, government regulations, and management complacency have served to point out that all levels of management, especially the supervisory level, must lead employees in ways that create, or help to create, climates where employees want to make a strong commitment toward achieving organizational goals. People, if managed properly, can be an organization's most valuable assets. The trend of declining profit margins will probably continue for the foreseeable future. The accounting profession has only recently seriously addressed the real costs of doing business. Costs, because of rigid accounting practices, are often understated. Managers at all levels, especially in many large industrial and commercial organizations, have become complacent because no one has, until recently, competitively challenged them; they will have to start learning to manage effectively again.

Countless arguments about the benefits and liabilities of unions have been put forth for many years. Unions are a powerful influence in most democratic societies. They are a part of society's institutional structure. In unionized organizations, supervisors must learn to work cooperatively with union leaders to help make the union's presence an asset. One real benefit of a union's presence in an organization is that it will force managers at all levels to be better managers, or pay the price of ineffectiveness in costly grievance settlements, arbitration, and restrictive labor-management agreements. In nonunion organizations, supervisors must recognize why people join unions, and, if it is within the. scope of their authority, not create incentives for employees to seek union representation.

Today's employees have more years of formal schooling than their predecessors, and they are also more exposed to information sources that may or may not be objective. Higher levels of formal education (although it is debatable as to whether workers today are any smarter than they were twenty years ago), have served to raise employees' awareness of what goes on around them and also to raise their expectations. Employees expect more from the work experience, and when expectations are not met cooperation does not come forth as readily. Supervisors must again lead in ways which meet employees' expectations. Problems occur when employees' expectations exceed, in large measure, organizations' abilities to meet them. Supervisors must also educate employees to understand the practical limits of what organizations can make available to them and why these limits exist.

It is apparent that the highly autocratic approaches to managing that were so commonplace a hundred years ago, to a degree, are no longer useful. In the short run, the authoritarian approach is highly effective. However, in the long run this leadership approach often produces negative results. Theoretically, the nondirective, or participative, approach is better than the directive, or authoritarian, approach. However, does theory work in practice? That is a complex question because many factors affect the success or failure of a leadership approach. Some of the factors and conditions that must be considered in determining if participative management can be successfully implemented are as follows:

• The technical structure of jobs allows employees to have flexibility in work activities. Some jobs in factories and offices are so structured by technology that the work must be processed in one way and one way only. In these cases, participative management is not applicable.

• Some jobs are potentially so dangerous that no deviation from standard operating procedures can be permitted. Therefore, participative management cannot be practiced.

• Some organizations, such as the railroads, government, and trucking, are so highly regulated that participative management's applicability is somewhat limited.

• Participative management can work only if employees are willing to assume responsibility. In many organizations, management does not want employee input in decision making, nor do employees want to participate in decision making; all they want is to do their jobs and be left alone. Within reason, they will comply with directions issued by others. Some employees may also lack the general or specific knowledge to make meaningful input to decision making.

• Unless high trust and confidence exist between people in the group, participative management will not work. The organization and higher levels of management must support this approach to leading. If one's superior refuses to support application of this approach, it will be difficult to put it into practice.

• Performance must be measurable; if it cannot be measured, the results obtained from this approach to leading cannot be determined.

• The organization's reward system must be geared to risk taking and goal accomplishment, and its discipline system must be geared to correct the behavior of those who do not perform up to standards or expectations.

Over the past 100 years, the body of knowledge about human behavior, in general, and behavior in organizations, in particular, has increased substantially. Managers are more knowledgeable about human behavior. The exception has been at the supervisory level and that is why, in recent years, books and training programs specifically for supervisors have been developed. Trained supervisors are better able to understand employees' behavior. Better understanding facilitates one's ability to avoid or resolve problems.

Acquiring Leadership Authority and Responsibility

Authority is the legitimate use of power. It is legitimized by some form of sanction given by society or organizations and their members. Authority carries with it a concurrent responsibility to use it properly. As the cliché has it, abuse or misuse it and you lose it. Power, in contrast to authority, requires no formal sanctioning or legitimacy. For example, suppose you meet a man in a dark alley who points a gun at your head and threatens to shoot you if you do not give him your money. Would you refuse and argue that he has no right to ask this of you? Of course not. While he has no legitimate right to rob you, he is able to influence your behavior because the gun in his hand gives him the power. Of course, you always have the alternative of not complying. However, the probable cost of noncompliance in this case is getting shot and possibly killed. This cost is usually sufficiently high to make most people comply.

In organizations, most applications of legitimate power or authority are accepted by members. When employees feel, for any reason, that authority is exceeded, they covertly and overtly seek ways to question and even resist the authority imposed on them. This is the use of countervailing power. Supervisors must always remember that they retain their authority only so long as its legitimate use is approved and its application accepted over time by the majority of those who are supervised.

Authority is usually vested in an individual, or the opportunity to develop it is sanctioned, by an organizational process. Authority, or its application, is a dynamic process that is affected to varying degrees by many factors. For example, as people, situations, or relationships change, authority changes. Authority is conferred (although it is rarely defined exactly as something one can or cannot do) by any one or combination of the following:

Function. This refers to the importance to the organization of the job and employees supervised. Such importance shifts with changes in objectives or operational constraints. In recent years, product design groups, quality assurance groups, and financial control groups have become more important to business organization's functioning. Poorly designed products that fail and cause loss of life or property are fair game for litigation. Because of declining profit margins and the increasing unpredictability of the future, financial control groups have gained more influence in organizational decision making. Other groups whose influence has increased markedly over the past ten years, are personnel, legal, environmental, and safety groups. Over the next decade, shifts in organizational power by function will continue to occur.

Position. Position, in this case, means the person's formal rank within the organization. Job titles and their meanings vary considerably among organizations. The title of president implies a different level of power from the title of supervisor. Titles like group leader, superintendent, director, chief executive officer, chief engineer, vice president, associate director, provost, dean, chairman, and manager all connote some degree of authority within the organizations where they are used. Position titles should be correlated to the relative level of power to facilitate employees' understanding of the range of authority and responsibility implicit in any title. For example, to most people, the title chief executive officer implies a higher organizational position and concurrent degree of power than the title assistant manager. If the reverse were true, it would confuse many people within, and most people outside, the organization.

Knowledge. There is an old saying that knowledge is power. People who have knowledge that is useful to the organization, or any individual or group, can share or withhold their knowledge as a way of asserting power. Supervisors must be somewhat knowledgeable of the work they manage. In some instances, supervisors may be the most knowledgeable members of their group. However, high levels of technical knowledge are maintained at the expense of managerial skills. Today, it is not uncommon for some employees in a group to have more technical knowledge of their jobs than supervisors.

Supervisors must recognize the power of the knowledge that employees possess. Dissatisfied employees who possess necessary job-related knowledge can, and often do, find ways of withholding knowledge to restrict cooperation.

Personality. People in positions of authority sometimes possess charisma. People inherit certain of their traits and characteristics and develop others. How we look, feel, believe, think, act, and react all change, in varying degrees, over time. People, based on their perceptions, continually assess the benefits and liabilities of relationships. The higher the degree of identification and attraction employees have to their supervisors, the more the supervisor is able to influence their behavior. In effect, supervisors are able to increase or extend their power because their traits and characteristics are perceived positively by employees. Of course, the opposite conditions could exist. Power based on charisma is quite fragile, because people's feelings, beliefs, and attitudes can change quickly. Supervisors can use their charismatic authority to supplement other sources of authority. It would be risky to use charisma as a substitute for other bases of authority.

Other Factors. Other factors affecting the development of a person's scope of authority would include: number of personnel supervised, worth of equipment under direction, size of budget, political support from superiors, and situational factors.

Authority: Acceptance and Resistance

Every supervisor at one time or another has observed that some employees will do almost anything they are asked to, promptly and without complaining. In addition, whatever they are asked to do will be done well. These are the types of employees that supervisors dream about. In some organizations these employees are few in number, while in others they are plentiful. Most supervisors, at one time or another, also have employees who do as little as possible and complain at every opportunity. When they finally do what they have been asked to do, they often do an average job. These two extremes have been shown for illustrative purposes. Everyone has observed, in different situations and under varying circumstances, behavior ranging within the two extremes.

Why is it that some employees always seem to be fighting back? Why is it that some employees always try to cooperate? There is no simple answer to these questions. Background, experience, values, situational variables, perceptions, diet, attitudes, beliefs, feelings, and even heredity all influence behavior. However, the process of employees' accepting or rejecting direction can be discussed in a general way.

Every person has within him what can be identified as an area or zone of acceptance of authority. These areas or zones are dynamic, and their size is influenced by all the factors mentioned above and many more. Figure 7 illustrates the concept of the zones for two people. Employee A has a wide zone of acceptance of authority, while employee B has a narrow zone. The zones illustrated for employees A and B can be the zones for a given situation, or they can represent an average zone observed over an extended period of time.

In the situation illustrated, employee A will accept, without some form of resistance, more direction than employee B. The difference in the amount of direction accepted without ques-

Figure 7. Zones of acceptance and resistance.

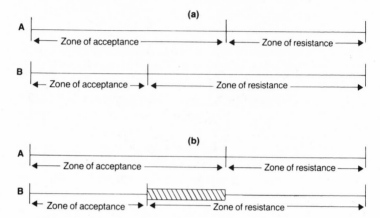

tions between A and B would be the difference in the width of the zones. The shaded area shown in Figure 7(b) illustrates the difference in the direction that will be accepted by A and B. Any supervisor would prefer to have employee A rather than employee B in his unit. Supervisors should avoid hiring employees who have narrow zones and would overtly and covertly resist any direction beyond the minimum to retain their jobs. Unfortunately, as discussed in Chapter 3, supervisors often either have little, if any, voice in the selection process, or they inherit many of their employees. In addition, zones of acceptance do not remain static. The effects of many factors will cause the zones to either widen or diminish.

The objective of supervisors is to develop within employees zones that are wide. This can be done by force—that is, fear, intimidation, harrassment, or cajolement—but this approach to widening employees' zones requires that the force be constantly maintained. As soon as the force is reduced, or employees develop stronger opposing forces, the zones will shrink. When employees voluntarily widen their zones, no force is necessary; supervisors need only maintain conditions that motivate employees to maintain wide zones.

Some supervisors erroneously believe that they should have employees with zones that are as wide as possible. The problem with employees who accept everything without question is that the supervisor does not get the feedback necessary to influence decision making.

Resistance to authority can show itself in a large number and variety of forms. When employees are motivated to resist authority, supervisors, in the long run, will lose. A supervisor may be able to outsmart or outmaneuver some of his employees some of the time, but he can never outsmart or outmaneuver all of them all the time. Employees have the advantages of time and, if many are involved, numbers. Besides, a tremendous amount of resources are wasted when supervisors and employees engage in this kind of conflict. Think of what could be accomplished if the antiorganizational creativity displayed by employees motivated to resist and retaliate could be channeled into cooperation and productivity. Employees motivated to resist and retaliate may spend the better part of their work day, and even time outside of working hours, thinking of ways to restrict, resist, and retaliate.

Following are just a few of the almost infinite ways in which employees can resist authority:

Forget to do something after being asked and hope that the supervisor also forgets. If caught, use defenses such as being too busy or not having time.

Comply to barest minimum possible, also known as marginal compliance. Next time, the supervisor might ask someone else to do it.

Argue strongly that it is someone else's turn when asked to do something they don't want to do. Claim harassment and discrimination if the supervisor persists.

After being directed to do something, go to the supervisor every few minutes and ask how to proceed to the next step.

Complain of illness and needing to seek medical treatment.

Take a day off from work when all employees know they will be badly needed.

Fake an injury or claim that an old injury has been aggravated by doing the job.

If a grievance procedure exists, file a lot of grievances over a short period and take considerable time to write or discuss them.

Overtly or covertly sabotage equipment or misfile paperwork.

Steal or conveniently lose something that is needed to maintain the flow of work.

The only effective way to deal with resistance is to identify the underlying cause(s) of such behavior and develop plans for corrective action.

In any organization, group dynamics exist. Formal and informal groups, in addition to individuals, develop zones of acceptance of authority. The degree of difference that may exist between the zones of supervisors, the employees, the organization, and the employees' friends or peer groups is important for supervisors to understand. Figure 8 illustrates a zone for the supervisor, the organization, an employee, and the employee's peers. Each zone differs in width.

In this example, the organization has the widest zone of acceptance. Keep in mind that an infinite number of combinations could exist. The zones decrease in size down to the employee, who has the narrowest zone. As shown in Figure 8, if the organization issued some directive at point A, the supervisor would accept it without question, since it is within the supervisor's zone of acceptance. Since the directive is also within the zones of the employee and peers, acceptance and

Figure 8. Zones of acceptance and resistance.

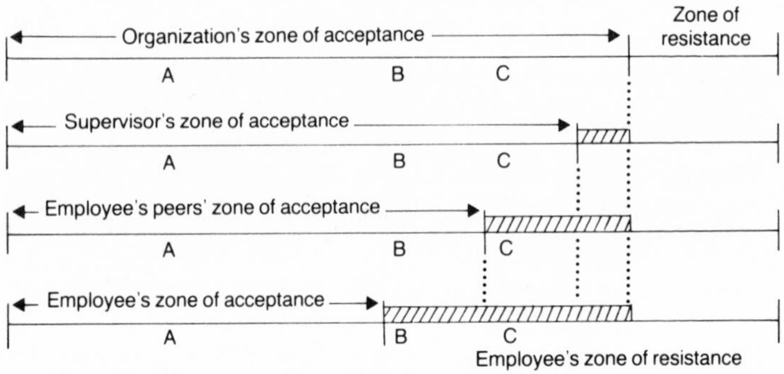

compliance will occur. Problems will start to occur when the directive issued by the organization, the supervisor, or both, shifts to point B, as shown in the figure. In this case, the directive is within the zones of organization and the supervisor. However, it is outside the acceptance zone of the employee. The employee will be strongly motivated to resist, but will not be supported by peers because the authority is within their zone of acceptance. If the directive is at point C, the employee will be motivated to resist strongly and will be supported by peers because the authority is outside of their zone of acceptance. This situation will inevitably result in a confrontation between management and employees. Either management influences employees to widen their zones to accept the directive, or the resistance of employees motivates management to shift the decision back toward point A or B.

Readers can develop any number of combinations to show the effects of issuing directives to others. The model shown in Figure 8 can also be drawn to show the effects of the upward movement of information. In these instances, information would emanate from an employee, or the group, and would be accepted as legitimate or illegitimate depending upon where it fell in the supervisor's and organization's zones. The ideal organizational environment, and one that should be the goal of all organizations, is to have boundaries of the four zones (employee, peers, supervisor, organization) matched as closely as possible. When this occurs, and if the zones are wide, the highest possible levels of cooperation exist.

Zones of acceptance are affected by the interaction of many variables. Some of the variables affecting employees' zones are shown in the following list. It is important to remember that the interrelationship of any of the listed factors, and the weighting placed on them, will vary greatly among people and according to general and situational influences.

Understanding of the nature of the direction employees are asked to accept.

Perception of the direction's consistency or inconsistency with employees' purposes and objectives.

Experience with the type of direction. What happened the

last time employees were asked to do something similar to what they are being asked to do now.

The perceived rewards for acceptance.

The perceived punishments for noncompliance.

Support from peers and friends.

Self-confidence.

Supply and demand in the job market.

Physical or mental health.

Perception of the credibility of the person issuing the direction.

Sense of professionalism and level of training.

What It Takes to Be a Leader

Is there such a thing as a natural leader? People are not born leaders. They may have inherited or developed traits and characteristics that motivate others to identify and be influenced by them. This phenomenon is a function of prevailing values and norms, which often change. Considerable research over the years has led to conclusions that people who exhibit certain traits and characteristics are more likely to succeed as leaders over the long run. The traits and characteristics of effective leaders are interrelated with the skill requirements for effective supervision, as outlined in Chapter 1. However, a number of distinct traits and characteristics can be correlated with leaders. These correlations can be made whether the leaders are formal, such as presidents and supervisors, or informal, that is, without organization title or sanctioning.

People who become leaders tend to have a stronger level of drive or perseverance than others. In the face of adversity or challenges, they persevere in order to reach a goal. Anyone who takes risk faces the possibility of failure. When failures occur, leaders are able to analyze and learn from the failure and renew their efforts to reach a goal.

Effective leaders are skillful in communicating. They are able to identify with and relate to those with whom they interact. They are skillful in applying verbal and nonverbal techniques to influence others. They understand human behavior and how to influence. They are able to create conditions or situations where people's needs are met by following the leader.

Another characteristic of leaders is that they tend to display high achievement drives. High achievers not only compete against the standards of others, they develop their own standards. In a sense, their need to achieve can only be satisfied for short periods of time. High achievers are continually looking for new opportunities and challenges. These types of leaders may be very creative and bring success to themselves, others with whom they interact, and organizations; they can be an organization's most valuable assets. However, they can also be an organization's worst liability. High achievers may exploit organizations and employees for the sake of personal gain. High achievers may also fail to recognize that they are different from other people and that other people may not be able to move at the speed and intensity that they move. This could lead to employees either withdrawing or rebelling.

Leaders display a high level of social and psychological maturity. This means that leaders not only know what to say and do, but how to say and do it. They have also developed an acute sense of timing; that is, when to say and do something. Many people have developed the skill to analyze problems and develop and implement solutions; but unless they know the right time to implement the solutions, they will not solve the problem. Supervisors who have had to negotiate, especially with union leaders in labor-management talks or grievance negotiations, learn to develop a sense of timing or they become ineffective.

Leaders display an ability to absorb and retain knowledge that is greater than that of followers, and they are usually more intelligent than those whom they lead. Intelligence and intellectual capacity, to a degree, are measurable. Standard IQ tests alone are insufficient. Intelligence is, in part, inherited. Intellectual development, however, is largely dependent upon stimulation, conditioning, practice, and reinforcement. Due to inheritance factors, one person may have a higher level of intelligence and even the capacity to learn more than others. However, if that intellect is not developed through stimulation and conditioning, its potential will not be realized. On the other hand, with proper stimulation, conditioning, practice, and reinforcement a person born with a lower level of intelligence could conceivably develop a much higher level than the person who started out with more.

Historically, societies have had a love-hate relationship with people who are more intelligent than the masses. Leaders at any level often find themselves simultaneously admired and respected, feared and hated. Leaders must be sensitive to the degree to which their intelligence arouses jealousy and fear among followers. It is well understood that the more inferior and threatened a person feels in the presence of someone else, the more he will try to avoid that person. If avoidance is difficult or impossible, nonviolent, or even violent, means may be used to remove the threat. Leaders should not hide their intelligence, but should be aware of how they display it.

Effective leaders have the self-confidence that allows them to take risks and accept responsibilities. Faceless bureaucrats, both in industry and government, tend to be risk avoiders and therefore avoid responsibility. As the late Harry S. Truman is reported to have said, "The buck stops here." Leaders, if they are to move forward, must be willing to assume risk and accept responsibility for success or failure.

Self-confidence is an important factor in a leader's willingness to make decisions. Decision making and responsibility go hand in hand. Leaders are the people who have to make key decisions. They must be able to absorb information, assess courses of action, weigh the risks, make the decisions, and assume the responsibility.

Leaders generally know how to conduct themselves when interacting with others. This does not mean a high level of social etiquette, although it does not hurt to have it. It does mean being able to control one's emotions without being unemotional. Joy, affection, tenderness, anger, resentment, and jealousy are all human emotions, and if they are not displayed, serious psychological problems may arise for supervisors and people with whom they have contact. The critical factor is knowing when, and to what degree, to display these normal emotions and feelings.

Another facet of effective leadership that is not often mentioned in management literature is a high level of moral integrity. Leaders set examples of behavior and are responsible for instilling a similar level of moral integrity in employees. The tragedy of Watergate and similar scandals are examples of the failure of leaders to have, and demonstrate through their actions, a high degree of moral integrity.

Leaders, particularly business and political leaders, must be able to function at a high level of moral integrity within the complex interrelationships of personal, religious, organizational, and societal values and prevailing law. They must also be able to predict and adapt to changes occurring in society.

Developing an Effective Leadership Approach, or Style

As leaders, supervisors develop and employ various approaches to directing the activities of others. They may learn how to lead by following the examples of predecessors or other leaders, or they may develop their approaches by trial and error. Observation, training, evaluation, trial and error interact to shape a supervisor's approaches to leading and serve as feedback in developing the approaches or styles that work over the long run. There is no best approach because the effectiveness of any style is a function of three general interrelated variables. They are: (1) the traits, characteristics, and needs of leaders; (2) the traits, characteristics, and needs of followers; and (3) a broad range of environmental and situational variables.

Some people enjoy controlling the activities of others, but the degree to which they have a need to control varies widely. People are attracted to leadership roles in structured organizations such as the military, paramilitary organizations like police and fire-fighting units, or the clergy because the structure, symbolism, rituals, and uniforms satisfy their needs to lead in a directive or authoritarian manner.

People with different personalities and temperaments are attracted to leadership roles in organizations such as some universities, think tanks, and research laboratories because the comparatively loose structure, informality, and less rigidly defined roles satisfy their needs to lead in a less directive, more collegial, or participative manner. Because leaders have different traits, characteristics, personalities, and temperaments, their needs to lead in various ways vary widely. To be effective, leaders must be matched to environments where the approaches or styles they are most comfortable exhibiting will work to bring about positive results.

Leadership studies conducted over the past 50 years have shown that some people respond better to highly structured work environments with directive leadership while others respond better to unstructured work environments and nondirective leadership. Again, experience, personality, training, and other factors interplay to affect a person's needs to work under either structured or unstructured leadership. It is important that people be placed in work environments and under supervisors who will satisfy their needs.

Leadership styles in organizations are also affected by a broad range of environmental and situational factors, of which the following are some examples.

The leadership style exhibited by supervisors, up to the chief executive officer. (In some organizations leadership styles depend on the length of the shadow cast by the person in the top position.)

The degree of structuring and control of decision making by organizational procedures, regulations, and rules.

The presence of a union and negotiated labor-managment agreement.

The level of danger present in the workplace.

The financial condition of the organization.

The organization's position in its industry.

The process of determining budget.

The supervisors' degree of responsibility and accountability.

The way in which work is scheduled.

Prevailing values, norms, attitudes, traditions, and past practices.

Legal constraints.

Technological constraints.

The degree of quality required in producing the product or service.

Size of the group.

The kind of behavior rewarded by the organization.

Leadership is too complex a process to be considered as just a function of a few variables. For this reason it is impossible to say conclusively that a particular style of leadership should be practiced by supervisors. What works for supervisors in one organization could bring disastrous results if applied in another organization. Leadership styles must be designed and tailored to fit.

Leadership effectiveness is broadly measured by the degree of cooperation supervisors get from employees in achieving organizational objectives within cost and time parameters. Supervisors can measure their own performance by comparing it to personal standards or expectations, organizational standards and expectations, or industry standards. Some of the specific performance criteria that should be measured are:

Quantity of production.

Quality of production.

Attendance of employees.

Degree of cooperativeness among employees.

Types and quantities of grievances filed.

Turnover of employees.

Cost of production.

Attitudes of informal group leaders.

Type and amount of upward communication.

Frequency of scheduled overtime.

Frequency of applying disciplinary action.

Degree of trust and confidence that exists between employees and management.

If the measurements of any one or combination of these factors do not meet, or exceed, the standards or expectations, supervisors must analyze the situation and determine the underlying causes of problems. Only then can a plan for corrective action be formulated.

Changing Leadership Styles

Supervisors, like most people, are creatures of habit. As such, they attempt to repeat behaviors that benefit them. However, changes in conditions, environment, or situation can necessitate changes in behavior. Supervisors do not always willingly change their behavior even when they recognize the need. Change can be forced upon people, but that can be a time-consuming and costly process. Long-run change can be best brought about if change is voluntary.

Suppose it is concluded that approaches to, or styles of leading need to be changed. How can change be accomplished? The following conditions are necessary to successfully bring about a change.

The most important factor in the change process is the desire to change behavior itself. The stronger a person's motivation to change, the higher the probability of success. Changing basic leadership style is not easily accomplished and can be frustrating. Maintaining focus on the objective is important. Directly interrelated with a person's motivation to change is the support they receive from others, especially superiors. Having a superior who will support, guide, train, and counsel you is highly desirable. A supportive superior can help you in the difficult periods and give feedback as to progress or the lack of it. Honest and accurate feedback is essential in achieving goals.

In developing a plan for change, you must recognize and accept the type of leader you are. Looking in the mirror is not very helpful, because we don't see ourselves as others see us. We are judged not by what we say, but rather by what we do. Once the self-deception is removed, strategies and tactics for change can be developed. Implicit in planning for change is knowledge of leadership and the defining of a goal.

As the plan for change is implemented, the rate of progress must be measured. Short-range goals must be set and standards of measurement developed. For example, reduction in complaints per month, increased cooperation, or increasing the number of meetings with employees can be criteria for assessing progress.

The rewards, both intrinsic and extrinsic, must be available and distributed as change in behavior occurs. Intrinsic rewards are the rewards people give themselves. Extrinsic rewards are the rewards given by others. Praise, recognition, compensation increases, and prestige are the types of rewards that should be available.

Last, when expected change does not occur, disciplinary action with the objective of rehabilitation must be put into effect. Without the ability to reward or discipline, changing people's behavior will be difficult to achieve.

6

Effective
employee discipline

DISCIPLINE is essential to all organized group action. The members of any formal or informal organization must control their individual urges and cooperate for the common good. In other words, they must reasonably conform to the code of behavior established and implemented by the organization, so that common goals can be accomplished.

The need to discipline, the development of effective disciplinary systems, and the proper application of disciplinary action are among the most difficult personnel problems confronting organizations. When the need to take disciplinary action arises, it is usually the supervisor who initiates the action and who may eventually carry it out. It is the supervisor who has the primary responsibility for influencing disciplined employees to change behavior. It is again the supervisor who must deal with the results of poorly developed discipline systems or the incorrect application of disciplinary action.

When people join an organization, they bring to it personal attributes, experiences, education, values, perceptions, beliefs, and prejudices. Because each person is unique, he or she views the world somewhat differently from everyone else. As we have discussed, when people take employment with an organization, they expect certain rewards from membership and participation. The organization also expects to benefit from employing people. Implicit in people's joining organizations is that membership usually involves some loss of freedom. This causes problems in any society where freedom and democracy are strongly emphasized and valued. For the most part, business organizations are something less than democratic in relationships with employees. Differences in job titles, compensation, working conditions, location of offices, positions on organization charts, and other so-called privileges of rank make it easy to see that all employees do not have the same rights, privileges, power, and status.

The amount of individuality or freedom people are willing to give up to gain the benefits from membership in the organization depends on many factors. What people are willing to give up—economically, socially, psychologically, or physically—is proportional to what they expect in return from the relationship with the organization. The more people feel that they are giving up, the more they will expect in return. If the rewards from organization membership and participation are immediate, employees may be willing to give up more. If the rewards are given in the future, employees will either give up less, or expect larger rewards because of time delays and risk taking.

In any formal organization, there are pressures that push the organization toward conformity and uniformity. There also exist counter pressures that pull the organization toward nonconformity and flexibility. The push-pull effect influences the formulation of policies, procedures, guidelines, and employees' behavior. Conformity and uniformity result in short-run high efficiency. However, individuality and creativity often suffer. Nonconformity, in the short run, results in inefficiency. In the long run, individuality and creativity may be high. Does this mean that organizations should operate on principles of nonconformity and flexibility? Not necessarily. Too much flexibility and nonconformity with no policies, programs, and procedures for guiding employees' behavior lead to eventual chaos. The results of chaos are collapse and failure. All organizations must develop disciplinary policies and procedures to maintain congruity and continuity. When disciplinary policies, procedures, and guidelines are vague or nonexistent, employees, because they do not know where the boundaries of acceptable behavior are, will experience anxiety and apprehension. This will lead to defensive or aggressive behavior.

When disciplinary policies or actions are perceived as being unfair, employees will develop feelings of injustice about the way they are treated. From earliest times, people have been concerned about justice and fair treatment. Feelings of injustice and a sense of grievance have been the underlying causes of most, if not all, revolutions. Managers, at all levels, must understand that when people believe they have been treated unfairly, they will, if the reasons are sufficiently strong, be motivated to seek revenge.

Dictatorships in an organization can survive only if they generate enough fear through police actions to quell thoughts, or actions of rebellion. Control by rules, regulations, severe disciplinary actions, and the like is expensive and time consuming and often at the expense of progress. Many Central American, Asian, and African nations are governed by dictators. Maintenance of a police state, in the long run, usually affects economic development and increases people's desire to overthrow the government. The same circumstances can arise in a business organization where management believes it is fair and just without considering employees' feelings about fairness and justice.

Justice, or fairness, has a very elusive meaning. What is just or fair is, and will continue to be, a matter of dispute in law, philosophy, and employer-employee relations. In the management of people, the development and administration of a fair system of justice is one of the most critical problems facing a supervisor.

Allocative Justice

Allocative justice involves a proportional allocation of rewards and penalties, whichever the case may be, according to policies, rules, procedures, and the facts and circumstances pertaining to each case. Each case, whether it involves a reward or corrective action, must be judged on its particular merits. A sum of money, for example, may be fixed in terms of the total available. However, it can be divided into parts and allocated on the basis of merit. Corrective action, on the other hand, has a relatively inexhaustible supply. The allocation of rewards, while partially fixed in supply, and the allocation of corrective action, while inexhaustible in supply, must be allocated in the same ways. They are given according to merit. Rewards are proportional to the available rewards. Corrective actions must be proportional to the prevailing standards, norms, and the facts and circumstances pertaining to a particular situation as compared to all others.

The concept of a fair system of organizational justice and its effect upon an employee's perception of satisfaction or dissatisfaction are interrelated with many variables within the individual and the work environment. Perceptions of rewards, penalties, privileges, status symbols, and opportunities interact to produce feelings of justice or injustice. For example, office workers today often earn less than factory workers. This has led to feelings of unfairness and dissatisfaction among office workers.

Whether or not these feelings are defensible is irrelevant. What one group perceives to be fair treatment, another may perceive as being unfair. The courts and arbitrators are backlogged with cases of perceived injustices involving compensation, promotions, demotions, transfers, layoffs, suspensions, and terminations. If organizations are to function effectively and efficiently over time, whatever rules and regulations are developed and administered must be perceived as fair by the majority of the organization's members. As noted, continued perceptions of unfairness or injustice can lead to some form of withdrawal or some form of aggressive behavior against the organization. Aggressive behavior can manifest itself as sabotage, absenteeism, turnover, unionization, arbitration, court actions, and other antiorganization behavior.

Organizational Due Process

Another aspect of justice is the mechanism of due process available to employees who believe they have been treated unfairly or improperly under the organization's allocative justice system. It is essential that all formal organizations have such a system for employees. Citizens of the United States and other democratic nations have their individual civil rights safeguarded. The United States has one of the most comprehensive due process systems in the world. Employees, whose civil rights are well protected, expect the same level of protection for their industrial rights. A formal organization that does not have a due process system for employees risks creating perceptions of unfairness and injustice.

In the absence of an organizational due process system, most employees, in time, will believe that either they or others have been treated unfairly. Authority to reward and discipline, without a system for reviewing and checking, is authority that will eventually be misused. History is replete with many examples of unchecked authority being misused. It is important to keep in mind that people react to what they perceive to be reality, rather than what is reality. Components of formal due process systems are grievance or complaint-handling procedures. All due process systems are designed to achieve the same goal; that is, to review the decisions and actions initiated by others to insure justice and fair treatment.

Organizational due process is necessary not only for those who are, or may be, directly affected; it is also necessary for managers who develop and administer the rewards and discipline systems. One very good way to measure supervisors' effectiveness as managers is to give employees the right to challenge their decisions. When supervisors' decisions are reviewed and supported by higher management, it is positive feedback that reinforces supervisors' behavior. When higher-level managers do not support supervisors' decisions, the feedback can be used to help supervisors learn from mistakes. This is part of the development of supervisors as managers.

The most common formalized system for administering due process is the grievance and arbitration procedure that exists in nearly all negotiated labor-management agreements. The main purpose of the grievance procedure is to provide a means for review and possible modification of the allocation of rewards and penalties. For all practical purposes, what is just or fair will be what is agreed upon between the union and management during the negotiations that take place at the various steps of the grievance procedure, or in the decision handed down by an impartial arbitrator. Many nonunion organizations have recognized the necessity and value of an organizational due process system. They have developed and implemented systems incorporating the spirit and philosophy of the system in effect in unionized organizations. However, one feature they usually lack is the availability of arbitration as the final step for the resolution of disputes. This deficiency has been partially overcome, with many pro and con arguments, in that employees can seek review of their perceived injustices through various governmental agencies and the courts.

Approaches to Discipline

Discipline provides a means, based on authority or power, to bring about a change in behavior on the part of an individual or group. Disciplinary situations arise when a person or group has violated the norms of acceptable behavior of that group or organization. Norms may be implicit or explicit rules of behavior or methods of operation. Implicit norms are more subtle and often more difficult to understand than explicit norms, which can only be inferred from the behavior exhibited by others in the group or organization.

Webster's dictionary gives three basic meanings of the word *discipline:* (1) training that corrects, molds, strengthens, or perfects; (2) control gained by enforcing obedience; and (3) punishment or chastisement. If meanings one and two are combined, it can be stated that discipline involves the conditioning or molding of behavior by applying rewards and penalties. The third meaning is narrower, because it pertains only to the act of punishing.

The first dictionary definition is treated to mean the positive approach. This is the kind of discipline that managers, at all levels, should strive to create. Positive discipline is actually broader and more fundamental than the dictionary definition "training that molds, corrects, strengthens, or perfects" implies. Positive discipline involves the creation of attitudes and an organization climate where employees willingly conform to established rules and regulations. It is achieved when management applies the principles of positive motivation, and effective leadership is exercised by supervision.

The second and third meanings of discipline encompass the use of penalties, or the threat of penalties, to influence people to obey orders and to live up to the rules of the system. Often force is employed. This kind of discipline was exercised by sea captains over sailors, pharaohs over slaves, and by military establishments. When development of a system of disciplinary or corrective action is indicated, wide varieties of approaches can be used. The approaches fall into two broad classes: a positive approach, which deemphasizes punishment, and a negative approach which tends to emphasize punishment.

Negative approaches to discipline

Under the concept of negative discipline, corrective action is carried out with the objective of punishing the wrongdoer so he will not break the rules again for fear of more severe punishment. Punitive action has a secondary objective of intimidating other employees so they will not break rules out of fear of being caught and subjected to similar punishment. The most common form of negative discipline used in business organizations is the so-called progressive discipline system. Under progressive discipline systems, the severity of the disciplinary action applied to the wrongdoer depends on the frequency and seriousness of rule violations. Figure 9 is an example of a typical progressive discipline system.

In unionized organizations, for valid and invalid reasons, management's flexibility in disciplining employees is often restricted by the negotiation process. For the most part, supervisors only have the authority to use progressive disciplinary action. It is unfortunate that management is so restricted because in many unionized organizations a high degree of mutual distrust exists between labor and management. Labor and management must share the blame for these conditions. Progressive discipline alone is ineffective with many employees, but it can be effective when used in conjunction with positive approaches.

On many occasions the author has observed a sort of boom and bust cycle in organizations where formal labor-management relations exist and progressive discipline is the only method employed to correct employees' misbehavior. Employees are taken up through various levels of progressive discipline, and then a crisis takes place when they are about to be discharged. This is especially true in situations where many are to be discharged within a relatively short period. Either the discharges take place, and are sustained through arbitrations, or they are modified because of the pressures generated by the union. In the latter case, the disciplinary system is worn down by the union. If this is done continually, management eventually finds itself without an effective system of discipline. Since positive discipline may not be allowed, managers will find themselves in a position of being unable to control employees who break rules.

In addition to disciplinary warnings and suspensions from work, many other approaches to punishing or teaching employees a lesson are used: ridicule, sarcasm, dirty jobs, compulsory overtime, harassment, threats, and intimidation. These approaches are dangerous, because instead of influencing disciplined employees to change their behavior, they often impel employees to want to get even, or seek revenge. Some approaches are even unlawful.

Many approaches, depending upon the intent and method of application, can be viewed as either negative or positive. When the action is taken with the intent to punish, it is viewed as negative; when it is taken with the objective of helping the employee to change behavior, it is viewed as positive. A positive approach is essentially rehabilitative. Some of the more commonly used approaches, which, again, may be either negative or positive in intent, are: transfer to another job or shift; demotion; discriminatory treatment, for example, raises, promotions, overtime, privileges; peer pressure, silent treatment; and changing work assignments.

As long as there are employees who break rules and do not respond to positive approaches, negative approaches will be used. Negative approaches will also continue to be used because some people derive a great deal of satisfaction through

Figure 9. Disciplinary action for specific offenses.*

Figures in penalty columns indicate regularly scheduled working days off without pay. "Warning" means a written warning.

No warning or penalty, with the exception of suspension, will be charged against an employee for over one year from the date of such warning or penalty.

Offense	First Offense	Second Offense	Third Offense
General Conduct			
Smoking in prohibited areas. (Locker room, shower or toilet)	Warning to Suspension	3 days to Suspension	Suspension
Reporting for work under influence of liquor Drinking on the job	1 day Suspension	1 week	Suspension
Fighting	3 days	1 week	Suspension
Horseplay Stealing	Warning Suspension	3 days	1 week to Suspension
Sleeping	Warning	3 days	1 week to Suspension
Loafing Insubordination	Warning Suspension	3 days	1 week to Suspension
Ringing other employee's time card	Suspension		
Malicious use of profane or abusive language to others	Warning	3 days	1 week to Suspension
Unauthorized solicitation or sales on Company premises	Warning	1 day	1 week to Suspension
Unauthorized distribution of written or printed material of any description	Warning	3 days	1 week to Suspension
Unauthorized posting or removing of material from Company bulletin boards	Warning	3 days	1 week to Suspension
Violating common decency or morality on Company property	1 week to Suspension	Suspension	
Garnishee	Warning	Warning	1 week to Suspension

* Courtesy of the Dayton Forging and Heat Treating Company, Dayton, Ohio.

Production and Attendance

Absence without notifying the Company or without reasonable excuse	Warning	3 days	1 week to Suspension
Work spoilage	Warning	3 days	1 week to Suspension
Destruction of Company property	Warning	1 week	Suspension
Interference with production of operations	3 days	1 week	Suspension
Failure to report a breakdown	Warning	3 days	Suspension
Failure to report work not to specifications or sketches, or spoilage	Warning	3 days	Suspension
Tardiness	Warning	Warning	3 days Suspension

Safety, Housekeeping and Health

Not wearing proper safety equipment	Warning	3 days	1 week to Suspension
Removing of or failure to replace guards	Warning	Warning to 1 week	1 week to Suspension
Misuse of sanitary facilities	Warning	Warning to 1 week	1 week to Suspension
Creating a hazard	Warning to Suspension	3 days to Suspension	Suspension
Failure to report any occupational accident, injury or illness within 24 hours	Warning to Suspension	1 week	Suspension

Miscellaneous

Falsification of records	1 week	Suspension	
Failure to obtain supervisor's permission to leave the job	3 days	Suspension	
Frequent loss of time. (Chronic tardiness or absenteeism)	Warning to Suspension	3 days to Suspension	Suspension
Refusal to do the work assigned	Suspension		

imposing social, psychological, and even physiological pain, anguish, and suffering on others.

Positive approaches to discipline

The philosophy underlying all positive approaches to discipline is that the purpose of disciplinary action is to rehabilitate rather than to punish. As noted, some of the approaches described as negative can be positive if they are administered under a rehabilitative philosophy. In positive, or rehabilitative approaches to discipline, supervisors develop in employees attitudes of adherence to necessary rules and regulations, or guidelines of organization behavior. Employees, as individuals and as groups, adhere to required standards of behavior because they understand, believe in, and support them.

Positive discipline takes the form of support and reinforcement for approved actions. This is fundamental to all learning. Corrective action for improper behavior should be supportive; there can be no vindictiveness. Supervisors let it be known that they approve of wrongdoers as people, but discipline them for specific actions.

A prerequisite for using positive approaches to discipline is communication of job requirements and the organization's rules and regulations to all employees. All employees must know when they are hired and thereafter what the organization and their immediate supervisor expects of them. The performance standards must be fair, attainable with reasonable effort, and consistent from job to job, unless differences in standards can be substantiated. The rules, or guidelines, must be reasonable and few in number. Supervisors must communicate to employees the kind of positive behavior expected of them, rather than dwell upon an exhaustive list of detailed prohibitions.

In creating a climate of positive discipline, supervisors must seek to build in employees a sense of personal responsibility and self-discipline. Supervisors apply principles of positive motivation and good leadership. Supervisors recognize individual differences among employees and vary methods and approaches whenever necessary. When employees are trained in their work and undertake to attain what is expected of them, they understand the limits of acceptable behavior. They know the rules of the system and where they stand. This helps them develop a sense of security.

Positive approaches to discipline are often akin to preventive maintenance. Some of the approaches used by organizations and supervisors are:

Counseling.
Reduced hours of work, or a flexible schedule.
High selectivity in hiring practices.
Proper placement of employees in jobs.
Probation rather than disciplinary suspension policy.
Training or retraining programs.
Shock reduction in disciplinary action.
Formal employee orientation and periodic reorientation for all employees.
Participation in formulating and applying rules.
Leaves of absence, with or without assistance of outside professionals.

Counseling must be part of almost all disciplinary actions, whether the intent is punitive or rehabilitative. Counseling as part of every supervisor's job is important enough to justify a separate chapter (Chapter 10) in this book; and it is an essential positive approach to discipline. Supervisors must counsel employees for the following reasons:

To find out if the employee who is being disciplined violated a rule or practice because of ignorance or intent.
To help the employee understand the importance of proper behavior and the possible serious consequences of improper behavior.
To have a record of the employee's progress, or lack thereof.
To support the supervisor's position if his actions are reviewed, or challenged.
To assess the employee's degree of remorse and desire, or intention of changing behavior.

If possible, allowing an employee to work on a flexible schedule, or reducing the number of total hours worked, can be very effective as an approach to rehabilitation. This approach is useful when an employee's disciplinary problems stem from overcommitment to other activities or personal conflicts. Many organizations have successfully used this approach to reduce employee absenteeism. However, because of production or customer service requirements, flexible work hours are not always possible.

Organizations and supervisors who hire the first warm body that comes through the door often end by hiring problems. The less selective supervisors are in hiring, the higher the probability that an undesirable person will be hired. Considering the job-rights protection many employees acquire after relatively short probation periods, supervisors often spend the better part of their day dealing with employees who should not have been hired in the first place. Organizations must decide whether they want to spend their money improving recruitment, selection, placement, and training processes or disciplining and eventually discharging unsatisfactory employees.

Many problems could be avoided if employees were properly matched to jobs. It is better to place an employee in a job that he can grow into, rather than one for which he is overqualified. Boredom, monotony, and frustration are often underlying causes for employee misbehavior.

Disciplinary suspensions may have outlived their usefulness in many organizations. The author has observed and heard of thousands of cases where employees who received disciplinary suspensions viewed the suspension as a reward rather than a punishment. This can be especially true when employees are compelled to work a lot of overtime. It is also true when the fishing or hunting seasons are open, or even when the weather is especially mild. If suspensions are viewed as a reward, employees will be motivated to break rules rather than abide by them.

Participating in a training program is usually viewed as a reward rather than a punishment. However, sending an employee to a training, or retraining program can be a highly effective approach to discipline. This is especially true if the employee understands that as a result of training, he is expected to change his behavior. The courts for many years have successfully used driver training classes as a form of discipline in lieu of suspending drivers' licenses.

Shock probation—that is, suspending disciplinary action or substantially reducing it—has been used for many years by the courts with mixed results. Supervisors should be cautious of using this approach to avoid setting precedents for similar cases. However, it can be effective in disciplining an employee in an effort to permanently change his behavior.

Employee orientation is an effective way to avoid creating disciplinary situations that may arise because of misunderstandings. In orienting new employees, the supervisor should explain what performance is expected and the help that is available to achieve it. Supervisors should discuss the principal standards of behavior expected of the employee, which normally include such things as good attendance, notification of expected absence, punctuality, good safety practices, cooperation with supervisors and fellow employees, abiding by prevailing standards of morality, and integrity. To achieve an environment where positive discipline works, all levels of management must set examples of proper behavior.

If supervisors take the proper actions to build cohesive, loyal work groups, they will find that group members will tend to actively support and augment their disciplinary efforts. To do this, supervisors must recognize the informal leadership that exists in any group. Supervisors can lead discussions covering organization rules and regulations, and employees can discuss how they apply in work situations. If the group understands and believes in the rules, it will often exert pressure upon its members to insure that they live up to the rules. In an informal way, the group can supplement supervisors' efforts in such areas as prevention of horseplay, achieving good attendance, not stealing property, doing a fair day's work for a fair day's pay, and controlling the length of coffee breaks.

Employees' acceptance of rules and regulations can be greater if they are given a voice in their formulation and application. This can be accomplished in group meetings where the supervisor encourages employees to agree upon the minimum norms of conduct that are believed to be necessary for effective and safe operations. In practice, management rarely involves employees in either the formulation or the enforcement of rules and regulations. Management, almost universally, considers discipline to be a management prerogative and responsibility, and is reluctant to share this responsibility with employees or, if a union exists, with the union.

People always have problems in their lives, and although they are usually able to cope with them, problems occasionally become overwhelming. When this happens to employees, they will often use alcohol or other drugs as a way of escaping the situation. However, the effects over time are usually disastrous. Since employees are an investment, it is good business as well as good personnel practice to try to protect that investment. Granting a leave of absence, with a recommendation to seek professional assistance if that is indicated, can benefit all concerned.

Discipline and Its Possible Effects on Employees and Groups

As has been discussed throughout this book, the informal social group can play an important role in the success or failure of personal relationships between supervisors and employees. Employees as a group develop their own values and norms, which often vary from the values and nors of supervisors and the organization. Employees can use their own reward and punishment system to influence one another's behavior.

When their cohesiveness is high, employees have a strong psychological and social identification with one another. If employees are disciplined by someone outside of the group, a supervisor, for example, the disciplined employees' peers may rally to support them. The supervisor may think that some form of discipline has been imposed that in some way will change the employees' behavior. Because of the group's support of the employees, however, the expected result is often not obtained. Peer support may motivate the disciplined employees to continue to break rules as a way of increasing their popularity.

Employees are knowledgeable of, and sensitive to, the behavior required of them by their peers, and they tend to fear the pressure that can be imposed on them by their peers far more than the pressure that can be imposed on them by their supervisor or the organization. Supervisors who find themselves in situations where their group's informal leadership is against them are in a precarious position. Any disciplinary action they might impose could be offset by rewards given to disciplined employees by peers. Supervisors must threaten, or actually carry out discipline that cannot be offset by rewards from the group, or convert the group's attitudes from hostility to support.

When a group of employees perceives that its supervisor is trying to split it up by transfers, layoffs, or even promotions, the group will tend to rally to increase its strength and maintain its security. The group will certainly try to make the supervisor's use of authority as ineffectual as possible. Supervisors must carefully plan how they are going to dismantle, or convert a hostile work group before action can be taken.

Supervisors must remember that when a disciplinary situation occurs and action is taken against an employee, future relations between the supervisor and the employee are on the line. At best, disciplinary situations produce anxiety and can be emotional. Whether the approach to disciplinary action is positive or negative, caution in handling the situation must always be exercised. If an employee is disciplined and reacts with some form of aggression, withdrawal, or apathy, future relationships with the supervisor will not have been enhanced; they have been diminished. Eventually, the deterioration of relationships will have an adverse effect upon performance.

What are some of the side effects of not handling discipline properly? When punishment is used as discipline, employees may show hostility, hatred, regression, or fixation; and as a result of frustration, they may use their creative abilities to figure out ways to break the rules without incurring further discipline. This situation arises all too often in many organizations. Employees will spend more time and energy finding ways to break rules than in trying to live with the rules or getting them changed through appropriate channels.

When the punishment is severe, for example, a long-term suspension, the employee may break the rule again, or may repress the desire to do so. When this happens, a strong conflict is created between fear and the desire to continue the behavior. The employee could become highly maladjusted, even be regarded as neurotic. The probability of neurotic behavior in employees increases when unjustifiable inconsistencies exist in the application of discipline within a group or organization.

Employees are just people, and as such they are influenced by their experiences, environment, home, family, community, friends, and jobs. Employees' perceptions of their work are peculiar to themselves and they function as a result of those perceptions, or cognitions. In effect, employees' behavior is a function of their environment, their perceptions, and their experiences, which can never be totally understood by others. From the discussion in this and preceding chapters, we can assume that, due to differences in people, conflicts are going to arise in interpreting required behavior on the job. Consequently, management's notion of consistent and fair punishment, as often written into disciplinary rules and procedures, may be unrealistic.

The specific use and the employee's specific situation must be analyzed within a broad framework. An employee's perceptions of given disciplinary situations are unique, and the justifiability and fairness of discipline is ultimately tied to the perceptions of that employee. Furthermore, each employee emotionally experiences feelings in ways that differentiate him from other employees. To one employee, discipline may be a source of motivation, to another, an inhibitor. To say without qualification that punishment is useful is a dangerous statement. Some employees respond to punishment in a manner that supports the traditional assumption that it is useful. Consequently, an evaluation of the usefulness of punishment as disciplinary action must be made according to the conditions in the organization and the particular situation.

Increasing the Effectiveness of Discipline

The first objective of discipline is to rehabilitate rather than punish. This does not mean that punitive actions cannot be taken. Punitive action, such as a discharge, can have the objective of helping the discharged employee learn not to make the same mistakes on the next job. The second objective of discipline is to fit the action to the seriousness of the offense, prevailing standards, and the employee's record and to carry it out in a way that will prevent, or minimize the probability of similar recurring behavior by the employee or others.

It is the responsibility of management to develop and communicate to employees the organization's philosophy of discipline. Definitive policies, procedures, guidelines, and rules must be written in order to put philosophy into practice. It is a long-established principle in employer-employee relations that management has the right to adopt reasonable disciplinary procedures and rules. However, it has also been established that employees, especially those represented by a union, have the right to contest the validity of any system of discipline and its various procedures or rules. It is important that any operating system of discipline be perceived as being fair by both management and employees. In developing and implementing a discipline system, management would be wise to secure input from all levels of the organization.

Because of the critical role of supervisors in the administration of any system, it is extremely important to define their role and train them in the philosophy of discipline, as well as teach them how to handle specific disciplinary situations. One of the biggest problems that plagues the application of discipline is consistency of action. Supervisors have feelings and emotions, and it is not unusual for supervisors to want to apply rules to fit their specific needs. This can lead to broad inconsistencies in the application of discipline, which, if not defensible, can weaken the system rather than strengthen it. Because of the need for consistency of action throughout organizations, and because employees will through due process seek review of actions they believe are unfair, many organizations tend to centralize considerable authority in personnel-relations managers, or other persons or groups having similar responsibilities. This can be dangerous, because personnel-relations managers and the like, while having good intentions, do not always understand the needs of supervisors and employees. Removing authority from supervisors diminishes their effectiveness with employees and restricts their development as managers.

The need to maintain consistency of action is not incompatible with the need to develop and strengthen supervisors as managers. How can both goals be met? Supervisors must be fully trained in the philosophy of discipline, guidelines for applying discipline, techniques of counseling, and organizational due process for employees. Supervisors should be given the authority to issue oral and written warnings on their own. In situations of a serious nature that require stronger action, supervisors should be required to consult with their immediate supervisors or the personnel manager before taking action. This not only insures consistency of action throughout the organization, it also prevents supervisors from taking unwarranted or ill-considered actions against employees.

All levels of staff and management, especially supervisors, have a responsibility to communicate the organization's personnel policies, practices, rules, and regulations to employees. This can be accomplished by face-to-face meetings, orientation programs, employee handbooks, and posting of notices on bulletin boards. Supervisors should also explain how the rules are commonly interpreted and applied. Organizational rules or directives and memorandums issued by supervisors and others should be reasonably related to the orderly, safe, and efficient operation of the organization. Regulations concerning length of hair or appropriate business attire will not be upheld by arbitrators, in unionized situations, or judges unless management can prove that such rules are necessary and satisfy the following requirements: (1) they are reasonably related to the orderly, safe, and efficient conduct of business; (2) if not enforced, they would adversely affect the organization's image; or (3) they are consonant with prevailing industry or community standards. When rules, except for common sense rules, have not been communicated to employees, arbitrators have held that ignorance can be an excuse for not complying. Accepting ignorance as an excuse depends on the specific type of rule infraction, and the facts and circumstances pertaining to the situation.

The principle underlying the American and British legal systems, that a person is presumed innocent until proven guilty, applies to nearly all types of discipline cases as well. The burden of proof is upon management to show that the employee is guilty of the alleged offense, and that the disciplinary action taken is reasonably related to the seriousness of the offense and the employee's record. In effect, management must prove just cause. Usually the degree of proof required is a "preponderance of the evidence," or "clear and convincing" proof. A higher degree of proof is frequently required when the alleged misconduct is punishable by criminal law, or is regarded as morally reprehensible. In such cases, the common law standard of "proof beyond a reasonable doubt" has been required.

In determining if just cause for disciplinary action exists, supervisors must conduct a fair and impartial investigation to determine what action is warranted and against whom it should be taken. In some cases, such as fighting, immediate action is warranted. The best course is to suspend the employees pending the outcome of an investigation with the understanding that should guilt not be proven, the employees will be reinstated and paid all lost wages.

Conducting a Fair and Impartial Investigation

In conducting an investigation, supervisors should make an effort to determine the employee's motives. Did the employee break the rule out of ignorance, or out of intent? The employee's motives will certainly have a bearing on the type of disciplinary action taken. The object of any investigation is to reconstruct the incident as accurately as possible. Failure to conduct a fair and impartial investigation means that some reviewing party, either internal or external to the organization, will either modify or rescind the disciplinary action. In conducting an investigation, supervisors should adhere to the five W's: who, what, when, where, and why.

First, who was involved? Have all the parties to the violation of the rule been properly identified? Second, what happened, directly or indirectly, and what rules were violated? Third, where did the violation take place? Fourth, when did it take place? Supervisors must establish the time and date of the incident. They must be certain that the time corresponds with the preceding who, what, when, and where. Fifth, why did this violation of the rules take place?

When conducting an investigation, circumstantial evidence should be kept to a minimum. Supervisors should avoid personality factors and make sure that accusations by one employee against another are supported by facts. Supervisors must be sensitive to the motives underlying one employee's willingness to give testimony about another employee.

Keep in mind that one objective of discipline is to administer it in a way that will minimize damage to future relationships. The disciplined employee must not perceive a connection between the punishment and the personal feelings of the supervisor. A disciplinary situation is, inevitably, emotionally charged, and the rule breaker will feel resentful, even if guilty. Supervisors are apt to feel angry or, at the least, righteously indignant. Offenders may often feel guilty, not because they broke the rule, but because they have been caught. When supervisors discipline employees, an unequal relationship exists in the fullest sense. An assertion of inequality is ego diminishing for the disciplined employee, and is apt to cause a rise in emotional tensions.

Conducting a Disciplinary Interview

How does a supervisor set the stage for a reasonably impersonal disciplinary interview? First, he must be in control of his own emotions. If he is upset, he should wait until he cools down. He may even talk with one of his peers or superiors in order to get a proper perspective of the situation. In reviewing the incident or situation, was the investigation conducted in a fair and impartial manner? Considering the seriousness of the situation, did the investigation produce sufficient evidence to substantiate the need to take disciplinary action? If the answer to both questions is yes, then the interview should be scheduled. Interviews should never be held in a public area; the best place is in a private office. The purpose of the disciplinary interview is to discuss the matter with the employee and listen to his side of the story before deciding what action to take.

The supervisor should not procrastinate in administering discipline. The longer a supervisor waits before taking disciplinary action after a known violation of a rule has occurred, and a fair and impartial investigation has been conducted, the more likely it is that he will get a "who, me?" reaction from the employee. Supervisors who procrastinate before taking action may dwell on the incident. This can lead to distortion of the situation which, in turn, could cause an overreaction to what actually happened. Overreacting will not enhance future relationships between the supervisor and the disciplined employee. Just as time can adversely affect a supervisor's judgment of the situation, it can also have an adverse effect on the employee. An employee who knows that he has broken a rule, and knows that he will be disciplined, will certainly experience some guilt, apprehension, and anxiety. Some supervisors occasionally use time to make an employee sweat it out before taking disciplinary action. This is wrong and an employee who perceives that he has been made to do so will be motivated to get even.

When conducting a disciplinary interview, the supervisor should, in clear succinct terms, tell the employee why the interview is taking place. The case against the employee must be presented in an unemotional way. The employee must be given the opportunity to explain the reasons for his actions. Remember, the employee is innocent until proven guilty. If the employee is not given the opportunity to tell his side of the story, justice cannot be properly served. If the employee does not present a defense when given the opportunity and at a later time attempts to do so, he has weakened his case. If, during the course of an interview, the employee presents information that differs from the facts at hand, a further investigation may be warranted. After the disciplinary interview has been concluded, the supervisor should review the case and determine the appropriate action to be taken. Under normal conditions, the total time, from the moment the supervisor learned of the employee's misbehavior, to the application of disciplinary action, should not exceed one normal scheduled work week.

Determining the Appropriate Action

All employees must be judged by the same standards, and rules must apply equally to all. This does not mean that the same disciplinary action must be taken with all employees who are guilty of having violated a particular rule. Disciplinary action should be consistent, yet it must be according to the individual situation. This statement appears to be contradictory, but it is one of the most critical and difficult things for supervisors and others to understand and apply in practice.

As discussed, under normal conditions, people do not want to always be treated the same. People want equal rights, but treatment according to merit. It is the responsibility of supervisors to differentiate among employees. However, as discussed, the burden of proving that discrimination between employees is valid and justifiable is nearly always management's responsibility.

An example of this important concept should prove helpful. Company X has a rule against stealing. If an employee is caught stealing, the disciplinary penalty can range from a written warning to discharge. Supervisor A knows that a number of employees are taking pencils, pads, pens, and other supplies home with them, but has decided not to do anything about it because in his mind it is not serious. Anyway, the employees do not view it as stealing.

Supervisor B has the same problem, but views it as a serious matter and, under the appropriate rule, takes disciplinary action. The employees in supervisor B's group become upset because of the inconsistent application of the rule against stealing. From the information in the example, there does not appear to be any justification for supervisor A's not enforcing the rule. An employee who is disciplined under the rule could charge discrimination because other employees who are known to be stealing are not being disciplined. This situation is very common.

This same example can be changed to illustrate the problem of consistent treatment among employees in a group. Supervisor B catches two employees taking pencils, pens, and writing pads home with them. Both employees have been in the organization the same number of years, and have nearly identical records of service. Neither employee denies the facts, and separately each gives the same reasons for taking the supplies. Supervisor B gives the first employee a written warning and the second employee a one-week disciplinary suspension. The second employee files a discrimination complaint, or grievance, against the supervisor; the employee would win the case because there appears to be no valid reason for differentiating the action taken against the two employees.

To determine the appropriate action to be taken when employees break rules, think of a concept of employees' organization bank accounts. People have savings accounts at banks or savings and loan associations and make deposits and withdrawals. Interest is earned on deposits. When the balance is zero, the account is closed.

Employees' organization accounts are conceptually similar to their regular savings accounts. They make deposits, earn interest, and make withdrawals. Their deposits could be: good performance on the job, accomplishment, tenure with the organization, good attendance, cooperation, adapatability to changing requirements, raises, promotions, recognition, and getting along with others. They may even make deposits for misbehavior, if the behavior is condoned for long periods by the organization. The deposits compound over time; in effect, they earn interest. They make withdrawals by engaging in behavior or activities that are in violation of norms, policies, procedures, or rules. Withdrawals, like deposits, also compound. Employees who continually violate rules withdraw from their accounts at an accelerating rate. Some employees build up very large accounts while others build hardly any at all. When considering how much of a withdrawal a disciplined employee is making from his organization bank account, a number of factors must be considered.

The facts and circumstances surrounding and pertaining to the disciplinary incident. Employees can give some very imaginative reasons for violating a standard or breaking a rule. The content and validity of the facts and circumstances must be evaluated and weighed. As an example: many organizations have a rule stating that if employees are absent from work for a given number of consecutively scheduled work days and do not call in to say why they are absent, they must be discharged. "Must" is a dangerous word to use in any rule. It normally does not allow for an exception to it. On occasion, the word can be circumvented by making an exception, and stating in writing, that the exception does not set a precedent for future cases. Better yet, use "may" instead of "must." If a high-performing, long-service employee is absent for the stipulated number of consecutive days without reporting, he would normally have to be discharged under such a rule. However, what if that employee had gone hunting and was stranded in the woods and unable to reach a telephone. Should the employee still be discharged? Of course not. The facts and circumstances show that the rule violation was unintentional, and the employee could not possibly have called in to report his reason for absence.

The seriousness of the rule that has been broken. Violations fall into two categories: major offenses for which an employee can be discharged, and minor offenses usually requiring something less than discharge. However, an accumulation of minor offenses can lead to discharge action. The questions to be asked and answered are: what type of rule was broken and how often has it been broken?

An employee's record of conduct. An employee with a record of infrequent or no rule violations will have that in his favor. Other things being equal, an employee who rarely breaks a rule is likely to be given the minimum penalty for a first infraction. If an employee has broken rules in the past, the length of time since his last involvement must be considered. Usually, after a period of time, an employee's record is wiped clean: past disciplinary actions are removed from an active personnel file and placed in an inactive file. The records should not be thrown away. Employees must be aware of the existence of both files. Access to files must be closely controlled on a need-to-know basis.

The employee's length and quality of service. A long-term employee with a good record of service would certainly receive a lesser form of discipline for a rule violation than a short-term employee with a poor record of service.

Mitigating or aggravating circumstances. Conditions on the job, relationships with other employees, changes in the level or type of work being done, health, financial or family problems to varying degrees affect employees' behavior. Every supervisor has the right to expect reasonable attendance and a fair day's work for a fair day's pay. If over a long period of time there is a consistent problem with attendance or quality and quantity of work, then, no matter what the circumstances, an employee could be terminated. However, in cases where the condition is not chronic, full consideration should be given to mitigating, or aggravating circumstances.

If disciplinary action taken against an employee could involve termination, replacement of the employee must be considered. Supervisors should never allow themselves to be in a position where an employee cannot be terminated because he is indispensable. While, for the most part, employees are responsible people, knowing they cannot be replaced could instill a belief that they are entitled to special treatment. The possible reaction of a disciplined employee's peers must also be considered. As discussed earlier, peers exert high influence on employees' behavior. The duration and intensity of these influences cannot be ignored by supervisors.

Whenever the balance of an employee's organization account reaches zero, the employee is at the discharge point. Violations of some rules, such as immoral behavior or major theft, are so serious that no matter how large an employee's account, it is wiped clean. Does a zero balance mean that an employee must be discharged? Not necessarily. The supervisor has the right to recommend, or actually discharge the employee. However, keeping in mind that the objective of discipline is to rehabilitate and not to punish, another chance may be considered. This is similar to making a loan to the employee's organization account. When loans are made, they should be in writing. The employee's commitment to repay the loan should also be documented. The form of the loan may be any one of the positive or negative approaches to discipline outlined earlier. Of course, the positive approaches are preferable.

Some employees will default on their loans. When this happens, they should be discharged. As discussed, other employees' reactions to the discharge of one of their peers cannot be overlooked in considering discipline. Martyrs are easily created. When people die or are discharged, which is organizational death, there is a tendency for others to speak of the deceased person's virtues and minimize his faults. When a supervisor recommends or actually discharges an employee, the reaction from the discharged employee's peers should be: "He had every chance," or "I would have fired him long ago," rather than "He was a good person and really got screwed."

Many employees for whom their supervisors "went the extra mile," or made a loan, repay the loan with interest. Think of people who were serious sinners and then underwent a radical change in behavior. Think of people who change religions or become born-again Christians. People who make such dramatic changes are usually highly committed to their new way of life. Some are overzealous. The same analogy can be applied to employees who have sinned repeatedly by breaking organization rules. Supervisors, through counseling and other forms of rehabilitative action, may successfully convert them. Converted employees can become zealous, even overzealous, toward their work and their supervisors. Such employees are far more desirable than those committed to causing problems.

In all situations involving potential, or actual, disciplinary action, timely and accurate records must be maintained. The individual or group who initiates the action has the burden of proof. Failure to maintain records weakens the case. The results of all disciplinary discussions must be in writing. Disciplined employees must be forewarned orally, and in writing, of the possible consequences of continued misbehavior. Disciplined employees must clearly recognize where they stand and what changes in behavior are required or expected.

7

Managing
employee absenteeism

EMPLOYEE absenteeism is one of the most pervasive, persistent, and challenging problems confronting organizations in the United States and many other industrialized nations. Employee absenteeism, as it is broadly defined, has increased significantly in recent years. It is costly to employers, consumers, employees who come to work, and the nation. With little doubt, absenteeism contributes to rising costs and inflation.

Many organizations fail to measure the real costs of absenteeism and erroneously conclude that it is just a minor annoyance. Some organizations recognize the costs, but apparently are resigned to accepting high absenteeism as they do not take meaningful actions to reduce it. To them, absenteeism is another cost of doing business that eventually will be passed on to consumers in the form of higher prices. Other organizations have become so casual in their attitudes toward absenteeism they do not even bother to measure its costs, or do anything about it.

Supervisors, more than any other level of management, recognize the direct effects of absenteeism on the organization and all employees. Supervisors also play an important role in reducing employee absenteeism. However, to be effective, supervisors must be trained, encouraged, supported, reinforced, and rewarded by higher-level management and staff professionals for their efforts to reduce employee absenteeism. When higher-level managers and staff professionals are casual about reducing absenteeism, while demanding high production and quality, supervisors become confused, frustrated, and eventually apathetic or resentful. It is only after absenteeism is accepted as a costly and serious problem that meaningful efforts to reduce it can be initiated and implemented. Before any initiated efforts can be put into action, absenteeism must be defined, measured, and its underlying causes identified and analyzed.

Defining Employee Absenteeism

At first glance, it appears that absenteeism can be easily defined: Whenever an employee is not at work, he is absent. This sounds like a reasonable definition. Some organizations use this definition, most do not. Definitions of absenteeism vary widely because of the variety of items excluded or included in various definitions or formulas. Some organizations include vacations, holidays, jury duty, military duty, and other excused absences in computing rates of absenteeism. Other organizations limit defined absenteeism to employees' failure to report for work when work is scheduled.

One of the biggest problems in defining absenteeism is the treatment of absences that are supported by a statement from a licensed medical practitioner, that is, a physician, dentist, osteopath, psychologist, podiatrist, or chiropractor. In general, defined absenteeism should include all lost time from work because of sickness, injuries, personal reasons, and whatever other unauthorized time away from scheduled work activities.

Absenteeism is usually expressed as a rate or percentage. Various formulas have been developed. Here are some of the more common formulas in use:

$$\frac{\text{Total number of man-days lost}}{\text{Number of man-days cost + number of man-days worked}} \times 100$$

$$= \text{Rate of absenteeism}$$

$$\frac{\text{Total controllable man-days lost}}{\text{Man-days worked (excl. overtime)}} \times 100 = \text{Rate of absenteeism}$$

$$\frac{\text{Number of man-days lost through job absences during period}}{\text{Avg. number of} \times \text{Number of}} \times 100 = \text{Rate of absenteeism}$$
$$\text{employees} \quad \text{working days}$$

$$\frac{\text{Total of absentee hours for period}}{\text{Avg. daily} \times \text{Number of days} \times \text{Avg. number}} \times 100$$
$$\text{hours for} \quad \text{during which} \quad \text{of employees}$$
$$\text{employees} \quad \text{survey is being} \quad \text{on the payroll}$$
$$\text{conducted}$$

$$= \text{Rate of absenteeism}$$

Each of the formulas illustrated has specific advantages and disadvantages. Whatever formula is used, it should be used consistently throughout the organization. A system of record keeping must be developed, and data must be compiled and analyzed. Many organizations who are seriously involved in reducing absenteeism use computers to compile, tabulate, and analyze information about absent employees' behavior to identify patterns, trends, traits, and characteristics.

Absenteeism is often symptomatic of other problems. Unless the underlying causes of absenteeism are identified and addressed, approaches to reducing absenteeism will tend to be cosmetic. Information about employees' traits, characteristics, attitudes, and values, as well as the frequency, duration, and timing of absences, can and should be analyzed on computers to help in identifying cause and effect relationships.

One type of absenteeism that is difficult to define and measure, and therefore does not appear in any formula, is psychological absenteeism. This is the type of absenteeism that occurs when employees come to work physically, but are mentally absent. While some jobs require only minimum mental attendance, most require moderate to high levels of attention and commitment. Employees who are psychologically absent make a minimum mental commitment to their jobs. This problem of psychological absenteeism is very common. It can often be observed among employees whose work output cannot be readily measured against a defined standard on a routine basis. These types of employees can come to work physically and create the illusion of looking like they are working. This is not to imply that all employees whose work cannot be readily measured are mentally absent. Such a statement would be unsupportable.

Employees whose work requires mental commitment, and whose output can be measured on a routine basis, cannot readily do the minimum and avoid detection. These employees usually resort to being physically absent to avoid any unpleasant aspects of their job or job environment.

Costs of Employee Absenteeism

In organizations where paid sick days are given, employees receive full pay while they are absent. Most employees view paid sick days as additional vacation that should be taken. Many organizations have "use it or lose it" policies that encourage employees to take off from work. Some organizations have policies of compensating employees who do not use their sick-day benefits. This practice has questionable merit because it reinforces employees' perceptions that paid sick days are an expected form of compensation, rather than a benefit to be used on an as-needed basis.

Whether or not a paid sick-day policy exists, absent employees' so-called fringe benefits are still paid in part or in full by employers. Vacation time, seniority rights, holiday pay, pension rights, medical and life insurance premiums, and other benefits continue to accrue, or be paid by employers. This has the net effect of raising costs that are not offset by increases in productivity.

When an employee is absent, and the absence was not expected, work had been scheduled for the employee. Management has a choice of postponing the work until the absent employee returns or having someone else do it. This could necessitate the scheduling of overtime. An employee may be temporarily transferred from one job to fill the job of the absent employee. The temporary transfer might be an upgrade in position. This practice is common in unionized organizations. An upgraded transfer benefits the employee because he has an opportunity to learn and perform higher-level job skills. However, it is costly to employers because of lost efficiency. Most half-trained, or untrained transferred employees will not demonstrate the same degree of skill and proficiency as the trained absentee. Lower production quantity and even lower quality may result. When absent employees are unskilled, or semi-skilled, losses in production efficiency are minimal. To offset possible reductions in quality, more frequent inspections may be required. This too increases the cost of doing business.

Some organizations solve the potential loss of production caused by absenteeism by hiring more employees than are needed, sometimes as much as 15 percent more. Ten percent is quite common where overhiring is practiced. Employees and supervisors quickly recognize that if everyone came to work, there would not be enough work to go around. To them, the organization is saying that absenteeism up to a certain level is expected, and accepted as being normal. Obviously, this practice increases costs of doing business. Overhiring must be kept to a minimum.

To avoid missing delivery dates, and possibly losing customers, overtime is often scheduled to maintain production dates. Overtime is an expensive approach to combating absenteeism. Some employees are creative enough to figure out how often they should be absent to generate sufficient overtime. Employees also learn to pace themselves when they know they will be on the job for ten to twelve hours or longer. In organizations where overtime becomes chronic, employees, to avoid having to work, develop real or imagined illnesses, fake or distort injuries, and even purposely break rules to get suspended from work. All of these, as can readily be seen, add to the cost of doing business.

Absenteeism taxes already overburdened health-care personnel, equipment, and facilities. Employees, to avoid disciplinary action, often visit licensed medical practitioners to get an excuse for their absence. These excuses are easily obtained and are of questionable validity in determining whether or not the employee was really sick. Employers usually end by paying for unnecessary office visits, X rays, diagnostic tests, examinations, and hospital visits. Eventually, increased payments for services by insurance carriers are passed on to organizations in the form of increased insurance premiums.

Another cost of absenteeism is the administrative expenses incurred in maintaining records, issuing warnings, and carrying out other forms of disciplinary action. Counseling meetings and the like take time and cost money. If counseling suceeds in reducing absenteeism, it is money well spent, but if it becomes an ineffective formality, it is time and money wasted.

Causes of Employee Absenteeism

The causes of employee absenteeism are multiple and complex; a major cause is society's attitude toward it. Over the past 30 years, work has become much less of a primary part of most employees' lives. People often identify more with activities outside of work than with their jobs. The productive use of leisure time has also increased. Many industries, such as manufacturers of recreational vehicles and tennis and golf equipment, have started, or have grown rapidly, in the past 20 years. The more satisfaction employees receive from nonwork activities, the greater their commitment will be to those activities.

Another major cause of absenteeism is fringe benefits that encourage rather than discourage absenteeism. For example, paid sick days, increased numbers of paid holidays, longer paid vacations, paid leaves of absence, extended lunch hours, and lowered eligibility for retirement all appear to communicate that time off from work is more desirable than time at work.

Employees' expectations of the rewards they receive from work also influence absenteeism. As their educational levels have increased, employees expect and wish to make more meaningful contributions to their jobs. At the same time, many jobs have become so structured and narrowly defined that they allow for no self-expression or creativity. It is difficult for employees to make a commitment to jobs that do not meet expectations, provide no real challenge, are highly structured, and provide no opportunities for individualism and self-expression.

Job dissatisfaction that can cause absenteeism often displays a variety of symptoms to which supervisors and others must be sensitive. Treating the symptoms will not correct the problem. Treating the underlying cause is the most effective long-run solution. Symptoms could include any of the following:

High turnover
Excess of grievances or complaints
Open or concealed sabotage
Theft
Excessive tardiness
Frequent and long breaks
Increased desire to have a union
Increased activity by a union
Quality and quantity of work problems
Indifference, withdrawal, hostility

When employees are either overtrained or undertrained for their jobs, it affects their attitudes and attendance. Overtrained employees find no interest or challenge in their jobs. Undertrained employees may experience anxiety, apprehension, and insecurity because of their inability to meet job requirements. For them, staying home and avoiding work is safer than going to work and facing the risk of exposure.

Poor leadership or supervision contributes to employee absenteeism. In groups where absenteeism is low, it is not unusual to find a supervisor who creates an atmosphere that contributes to free and easy discussion of work problems, takes the time to talk with employees about personal problems, holds group discussions, and who can be counted on to stand up for employees.

Characteristics of employees also affect absenteeism. Employees under 30 years of age often exhibit higher rates of absenteeism than other age groups. Their absenteeism is principally caused by life styles.

Some employees are absentee-prone. They react to stress and tension by withdrawal. These patterns can be identified by tracing their absenteeism records with previous employers and throughout school years. Some employees are also accident-prone, which often results in absence from work.

Lack of a sense of responsibility among employees is another factor in absenteeism. When employees possess or develop a sense of responsibility to their jobs, fellow employees, and supervisors, they will be absent less frequently. Responsibility is not something that can be imposed on employees; it must be voluntary.

Lack of cohesiveness among employees, factionalism, personality conflicts, parochialism, nepotism, and dissension all contribute to absenteeism. To avoid these stresses and tensions, employees can and do develop virtually unlimited reasons and excuses for their absences to avoid conflict and possible disciplinary action.

Other causes of absenteeism directly related to the job environment are:

Excessive hours	Job fatigue
Shift rotation	Unclear responsibilities
Excessive heat	Erratic production schedules
Poor ventilation	Thursday paydays
Excessive danger	

Factors not directly related to the job or the job environment are:

Too much personal business
Moonlighting
Drug addiction
Marital problems
Illness or injury of the employee or his family
Child care conflicts
Weather conditions
Transportation problems
Inconvenient shopping and banking
Care of parents or relatives
Religious beliefs
Legal, economic, or social problems

Looking for another job
Medical problems such as dental, glasses, hearing aids, prostheses
Conflicts with leisure activities

The degree to which any one or combination of these factors causes or affects absenteeism can be determined only by analysis of absenteeism patterns.

Approaches to Reducing Employee Absenteeism

Defining absenteeism and analyzing records to identify cause and effect relationships are steps that must be taken before any approach or program can be initiated and implemented. As a result of record analyses, it is not unusual to find that 10 percent of the employees may account for 50 percent or more of the total absenteeism. This 10 percent often shares similar traits and characteristics.

Too frequently, management is content to stay within industry or geographic area averages. The feeling is that it is okay to be the same as others so long as they are not worse. Within average limits is where the organization wants to be located, but average organizations tend to remain so in all respects. Reducing absenteeism below averages reduces costs and increases profits.

A two-pronged approach must be used in reducing absenteeism. Higher-level managers and staff professionals must develop and implement programs and procedures; supervisors, with assistance as needed, must work directly with problem employees and insure that the approaches initiated by higher management and staff are properly implemented. Timely feedback must be given by supervisors to assess the effectiveness of approaches being used.

It is difficult and often impossible for organizations to compete with leisure activities. A picnic or a nice spring day is more satisfying than working at a machine in a factory, or at a desk in an office. Not all jobs can be made interesting, challenging, or satisfying. Some jobs are mundane, monotonous, and boring. Proper recruitment, orientation, selection, and placement of employees can reduce some job dissatisfaction problems. Flexible transfer and job-bidding policies help in placing employees in the proper jobs. It is important to understand that not all employees want interesting and challenging jobs. It is also important to understand that what is interesting and challenging to one person may be boring to another. Supervisors are often in the best position to find out about employees' abilities, expectations, fears, needs, and aspirations.

Organizations must establish attendance standards. It is the supervisor's responsibility to communicate those standards to employees. Standards of attendance and job performance should be communicated during orientation and reinforced periodically. Failure to establish, communicate, and enforce standards will result in employees establishing their own standards. What employees define as good attendance and what organizations define as good attendance can vary widely. Differences in perceptions result in problems.

Young employees, in particular, need to understand that accepting responsibilities is implicit in being an adult and an employee. Young employees often do not understand the seriousness or the consequences of absenteeism. A number of studies have shown that many young employees have little understanding of the effect that poor attendance has on their work, peers, themselves, and the organization. Supervisors, with the assistance of staff professionals, must teach young employees the need for good work habits and attendance.

Supervisors, through the use of rewards, can reinforce good attendance behavior of employees. Preferred treatment and privileges such as preference on being offered overtime, choice work assignments, occasional time off from work without penalty, recognition, status, larger raises, and quicker promotions, are all rewards that supervisors can distribute on the basis of merit.

Counseling problem employees is another approach that must be used by supervisors. When employees are absent or late for work, supervisors should meet with them privately or in groups, to find out why, and should keep accurate and complete records of the counseling session. With complete records of absenteeism and counseling, supervisors can measure progress, or lack thereof. If sufficient progress is not being made, other actions, including referring employees to the personnel or medical departments, can be considered.

In a unionized organization, the union should participate in counseling problem employees and must support management's efforts. Support and participation will be forthcoming only if the union understands the cost of absenteeism to its members—how it affects wages, benefits, and job security. Rhetoric about its effect on profits and production will fall on deaf ears.

Another preventive approach to employee absenteeism is the training of supervisors. Most supervisors, as has been discussed throughout this book, are not given the necessary training to be effective managers. Untrained or poorly trained supervisors will try to avoid problems rather than confront them. Supervisory training programs that are objective oriented, properly organized, staffed, conducted, and evaluated are essential. Learning put into practice must be appropriately rewarded.

Effective supervisors build cohesive work groups where employees develop high levels of mutual respect, trust, and confidence. When employees get along with one another, they are more motivated to come to work. When back stabbing or character assassination exists, it is safer for employees to stay home. Peer influence is highly effective in influencing an employee's behavior; employees can coach and counsel each other to overcome problems.

Supervisors can play an important role in determining the need to schedule overtime. Supervisors, more than most, know the adverse effects of too much overtime. They can inform higher management when overtime is causing too many problems among employees. A possible problem exists when supervisors themselves are paid overtime. Some supervisors, in order to earn additional income, will create situations where overtime is necessitated. In other cases, supervisors who do not want to work overtime, even though they are paid overtime wages, will manage to minimize the need for overtime scheduling.

When employees participate in decision making and develop a sense of responsibility to their jobs, peers, and the organization, they are less apt to be absent. Supervisors have a responsibility to help employees develop a sense of personal identification with their work and other employees.

A formal program in which supervisors are trained to identify potential and existing employees' problems is important for reducing absenteeism. Remember, absenteeism is usually symptomatic of other problems. Supervisors trained in counseling techniques can help employees to help themselves. In serious cases, supervisors should refer employees to staff specialists. Many organizations have on their staffs psychologists and psychiatrists, or other professionals trained in industrial medicine. In small and large organizations, liaisons with independent medical and social specialists can be easily established.

Some absenteeism is caused by physiological problems. A medical department staffed with licensed physicians and nurses, or a referral program to an independent medical group, is valuable in resolving absenteeism problems. Again, supervisors should have some basic training in being able to spot possible physical problems. Many employees fear physicians and hospitals. A supervisor who suspects that an employee's absenteeism is caused by a mental or physical problem can help the employee overcome his fears and seek medical attention.

Whether or not a particular approach to reducing absenteeism can be implemented, or will work, depends on many variables that cannot be adequately discussed in the space of one chapter. The following approaches are offered for general consideration.

Flexible work schedules. Many organizations have implemented flexible work schedules that permit employees to work long hours one day, and short hours another. If it would not hamper production or customer service requirements, such schedules should be seriously considered. A number of organizations have used four ten-hour workday schedules with good results. However, in some cases the benefits have been short lived, and absenteeism has even increased because employees have taken second jobs.

Child-care centers. With the increasing number of single parents and married women with young children pursuing full-time careers, some organizations are establishing child-care centers.

Work-incentive programs. Although they are not always feasible or practical, such arrangements, or assignments of piece work, can be useful in reducing absenteeism.

Physical checkups. Requiring semi-annual or annual physical exams for all employees can be an effective method of identifying ailments or disease that will eventually cause absenteeism.

Safety measures. Maintaining a safe and environmentally healthy workplace with sponsored safety training programs can play an important role in reducing absenteeism.

Health bonuses. A number of organizations have paid bonuses to employees who stop smoking. The links between disease and smoking are well established, and employees who do not smoke tend to be healthier than those who smoke. Healthy employees are absent less often than unhealthy employees.

Fitness programs. In recent years, Americans have put more time, energy, and money into physical fitness. Physically fit employees are less prone to illness, and when ill regain their health more quickly. Sponsored physical fitness programs and recreational activities are popularly used approaches to reducing absenteeism.

Cash incentives. Bonus and cash award programs for good attendance have been used to reduce absenteeism. While their intent is good, they tend to fail in the long run. Employees who normally maintain good attendance receive an additional reward which doesn't change their attendance habits. Chronically absent employees, if motivated by money, would come to work regularly and be compensated. In the author's opinion, a cash bonus or some other reward, such as a gift certificate, will not be a sufficient incentive to motivate chronically absent employees to come to work regularly.

Accrued sick days. Organizations that provide paid sick days for employees find it nearly impossible to reduce or terminate this benefit when it is abused. Many organizations have abandoned the "use it or lose it" philosophy and either pay employees for such days not used or allow them to carry their accrued days over into other years. Employees who remain employed with the organization for some stated number of years and then voluntarily leave employment may be paid for part or all of their accrued sick days.

Attendance Control Programs

When positive approaches to reducing absenteeism fail, management must resort to control programs that employ punitive, progressive disciplinary action. Punitive approaches, while not the most desirable, are sometimes the only approaches that will work. Fear and punishment on occasion can be very effective influencers of behavior.

Progressive discipline for excessive or chronic absenteeism is usually in the form of warnings, suspensions from work, probations, and eventually discharge. In many programs, penalty points are given to employees for tardiness, part-day absences, and full-day absences. Formulas for accruing penalty points vary widely. Absences that are considered excused and not counted against the employee's record for disciplinary purposes also vary widely. Some programs use credit points for good attendance to offset penalty points for poor attendance.

Because employees can easily obtain medical excuses for alleged illnesses, many attendance control programs count absences supported by a medical statement against an employee's record. Absences supported by a medical excuse may not be counted as heavily as absences unsupported by a medical excuse.

Whatever system of control is used, it must be reasonable and fair. Reasonable and fair are elusive words, and what is reasonable and fair for one group may not be for another. Specific conditions in the organization, industry, and geographic area and societal norms must be taken into consideration.

As employees accrue penalty points, they receive disciplinary action. The more points accrued within a specific time period, the more severe the disciplinary action. Figure 10 illustrates a typical program.

Discipline and Chronic or Excessive Absenteeism

Arbitrators and the courts have upheld employers' rights to discharge employees who for any reasons, including legitimate illness or injury, consistently fail to meet reasonable minimum attendance standards. The problem has been in determining when absenteeism is excessive. No general rules can be stipulated, but following are some considerations:

The employee's past attendance record.
The employee's length of service.
The employee's quality of service.
Clearly communicated attendance policies.
Fair policies applied fairly and consistently.
Sincere effort on management's part to determine if the problem can be corrected by action other than discharge.
Adequate warning to the employee of the seriousness of the situation and the possible consequences for failure to change behavior.
It can be shown that the employee, because of his condition, is unable within a reasonable period of time to meet minimum job requirements.

While it is always difficult to discharge an employee who has a legitimate illness or injury, management has an obligation to take such action against those employees who cannot meet minimum attendance standards. While to some people this may appear to be unfair, it must be remembered that organizations, and in particular business organizations, have an obligation to remain profitable and survive in order to continue serving society's needs. This is why social security, disability

Figure 10. Company attendance rules.*

It is the responsibility of all employees to report to work when scheduled. However, on occasion, circumstances will create situations whereby employees will be tardy or absent. These attendance rules make allowance for a reasonable amount of tardiness and/or absence and provide for progressive discipline for excessive tardiness and/or absence.

Absence not counted *toward progressive discipline*

Vacations	Funeral leave
Holidays	Attendance at a legal pro-
Jury duty	ceeding as required by
Military duty	a subpoena
Disciplinary suspension	Leave of absence
	Emergency shutdowns

Any employee who is absent for any one of these reasons, and who desires that the absence not be considered as an absence occurrence, must present satisfactory evidence to substantiate his claim within one week after he returns to work. If the employee does not present evidence within the one-week limit that he was absent for one of these reasons, each day of absence will be counted as an absence occurrence, and the accrued penalty points will be counted for his record toward disciplinary action.

Absence counted *toward progressive discipline*

1. One penalty point will be given for each full day of absence unless the reason for the absence is listed in the Not Counted group and satisfactory evidence to substantiate the claim is submitted within the one-week time limit.

2. One-half penalty point will be given for a partial day, full day, or continuous absence for claimed illness or injury, whether or not it is work related, if a doctor's excuse substantiating the claimed illness or injury is submitted. Medical excuses covering the period of absence must be submitted within one week after returning to work or each day of absence will be converted to one penalty point for each day of absence.

3. One-half penalty point will be given for each partial absence (reporting late and/or leaving early) that is over 30 minutes but less than one-half of the employee's scheduled shift.

4. One-quarter penalty point will be given for each tardiness (reporting late and/or leaving early) that is less than 30 minutes. No points will be given for tardiness that is less than three minutes after the start of the employee's scheduled shift.

* Adapted from various absenteeism management programs developed by the author.

Credits

Credits will be given to employees at the rate of one per month for each of the twelve months in a calendar year. The one credit that is given to an employee at the start of each month can be used during the same month in which it was given to reduce one penalty point from the total points an employee may accrue during the same month because of absence or tardiness, etc.

Progressive Disciplinary Steps

1. A total of four penalty points will subject the employee to counseling and a written warning.

2. A total of eight penalty points will subject the employee to a second written warning with a three-workday disciplinary suspension.

3. A total of 12 penalty points will subject the employee to a third written warning with a one scheduled work week disciplinary suspension.

4. A total of 16 penalty points will subject the employee to a fourth written warning suspending him for five days with intent to discharge.

Each written warning will stay on an employee's record for one year from the date that the warning was written. When a warning expires, the four penalty points associated with the warning will be deleted from the employee's accrued penalty points as of that date.

---

retirement, vocational rehabilitation, sickness and accident benefits, worker's compensation, welfare, unemployment compensation, medical insurance, and other benefits are provided for employees by business and government. They reduce the hardships caused by unemployment.

Before a good employee who has a legitimate medical problem is discharged, an effort should be made to place the employee in a job he can perform. If this is not feasible, progressive discipline should not be used, because warnings, suspensions, and the like will not correct the employee's problem. The discharge should be an administrative or medical termination rather than a disciplinary termination.

Discipline and Absenteeism for Unusual Reasons

Arrest and confinement. On occasion, employees break the law and are arrested. Arrest often results in confinement to jail. Sentencing by a court for crimes committed usually means confinement to jail for some minimum length of time. Employees whose absences are caused by their being in jail are subject to disciplinary action. In considering what disciplinary action should be taken, the same factors as considered for other types of absences must be considered.

Religious beliefs. The right to discipline employees who are absent for religious beliefs is affected by the ban on religious discrimination in Title VII of the Civil Rights Act and by state Fair Employment Practices laws. The Equal Opportunity Commission's guidelines call for employers to make reasonable accommodations to the religious beliefs of employees when it can be done without causing undue hardships to the organization or other employees.

Personal business. If an employee's absenteeism is not excessive, it is a good policy not to violate an employee's privacy by inquiring into his specific reasons for absence due to claimed personal business. However, if an employee has a record of excessive absences, the supervisor can require reasons and assess their validity in determining whether or not the employee should be excused or unexcused.

Absence on a scheduled overtime day. It is a generally accepted principle that employers have a right to schedule reasonable amounts of overtime. What is reasonable is subject to many considerations. In unionized organizations, labor-management agreements usually stipulate specific distribution procedures and limitations on overtime work. Employees who refuse to work reasonable amounts of overtime, or do not report for work when they have accepted overtime work, are subject to disciplinary action.

Tardiness or lateness; leaving work early. Excessive lateness and leaving work early, like excessive absence, cause problems. Employees who are excessively late, or frequently leave work early cause production and interpersonal relationship problems. They are subject to disciplinary action. Any rules or standards regarding lateness or leaving work early must be reasonably related to the operational environment of the organization and the needs of customers.

Before disciplinary action is taken, a sincere effort to identify and treat the underlying causes should be made by supervisors. Lateness and leaving work early, like absence, are often symptomatic of other problems. Keep in mind that if an employee is worth rehabilitating, it is better to rehabilitate the employee rather than discharge him.

8

Resolving
employee complaints

ON reading the title of this chapter, the first thought that will come to some readers is, "What about employees' grievances?" It is with specific purpose that the word grievance does not appear in the title. This is because no real distinction can be made between a complaint and a grievance. In essence, complaints and grievances are the same.

Organizations with unions and collective bargaining agreements sometimes develop classifications of employee complaints. Specific types of complaints, technically called grievances, are normally covered in negotiated labor-management agreements. They are eligible to be discussed under a negotiated grievance procedure. Other types of complaints, not specified in a negotiated labor-management agreement, are called complaints or gripes and may or may not be subject to a formal reviewing procedure. Complaints specifically defined as grievances are eligible for arbitration, which is the process whereby a person or group from outside the organization and the union is selected by the parties to hear and settle the grievance. The arbitrator's decision is usually final and binding on the parties to the grievance. Over 95 percent of all negotiated labor-management agreements contain a grievance procedure terminating in final and binding arbitration.

In mature stages of formal labor-management relationships, no attempts are made to segregate complaints and grievances. Management and labor have recognized that all complaints are grievances. Attempts to distinguish between complaints, gripes, issues, and grievances cause more problems than they resolve.

Government, in particular the federal government, often has overlapping, and at times conflicting, complaint-handling procedures. Employee complaints may be handled under any one or combination of the following procedures:

Civil service grievance procedure
Agency grievance procedure
Civil service appeals procedure
Agency appeals procedure
Negotiated labor-management grievance procedure

Multiple and overlapping complaint resolution procedures can be an administrative nightmare and a source of frustration to employees and managers.

Some organizations operate under the naive belief that a formal grievance procedure is unnecessary. Complaints are either assumed to not exist or are handled under what is commonly referred to as the open-door policy. As most supervisors know, a policy where employees can always go directly to the president with their complaints is disastrous. The first thing that results from this approach to handling employee complaints is that the relationship between the supervisor and the employee starts to deteriorate. Open-door policies can be very effective only if the door at the supervisor's level is wide open and the door at the president's level is slightly open.

Organizations that have no formal system or procedure whereby employees can seek successive reviews of their complaints are courting disaster. Complaints that go unresolved usually do not go away. They tend to fester like an open wound, and often lead to more serious problems. Some organizations have an informal procedure, but it is often vague and is usually misunderstood by supervisors and employees. The author has worked with organizations who use suggestion-type programs as complaint-handling procedures. Suggestion programs can supplement a complaint-handling procedure, but never substitute for it. Complaint-handling procedures need to be specifically defined and communicated in total to all employees.

The Causes of Employees' Complaints

Employees' complaints may have one or many causes and may be general or specific in nature. Complaints may stem from conditions on the job, outside of the job, the job environment, or within the employee himself. The long-run solution to resolving employees' complaints is to identify and treat the underlying causes. Complaints, like discipline, absenteeism, and other misbehavior, may be symptomatic of deeper-rooted problems. The supervisor plays an important, if not the key role, in resolving employees' complaints.

Supervisors, other levels of management, and staff professionals need to learn to identify some of the more common causes of employees' complaints. As noted, complaints are inevitable when people live or work together. Complaints can be channeled into constructive results, or they can destroy relationships and organizations. The author has worked with many groups where destructive conflict had reached the point of causing the organization to lose profits, miss opportunities, and face the real possibility of going out of business.

Top management makes personnel policies, and supervisory management carries them out in the workplace. Poor policies mean poor results. Good policies with poor implementation also mean poor results. Traditions, past practices, prejudices, insensitivity, and ignorance in top management usually underlie the cause of poor policies and practices. Poor selection, improper or no training, insensitivity, prejudice, and insecurity often underlie supervisors applying policies incorrectly. From these conditions, complaints arise.

In an era where people tend to think that everyone must be

treated the same, the fact that some lead and others follow is a cause for complaint. Some supervisors are power hungry. They enjoy commanding in the full sense of the word. They like to think of themselves as old-time drill corps sergeants. Some employees, as is well understood, resent and object to any type of authority. Either type of situation serves to generate complaints.

Communications problems interrelated with values, education, role, culture, age, ethnic origin, sex, and race differences, can all be sources of complaints. Sometimes employees complain just to find out what is going on. When management fails to keep employees informed, employees' level of curiosity tends to increase. Curiosity may be tinged with suspicion, insecurity, or mistrust. Complaining is one way to find out from management what is going on in the organization. Employees will also complain to test their perception of a communication's meaning, or to test the validity and intent of the communication.

In a unionized environment, the union and its leadership play key roles in generating, pursuing, and resolving employees' complaints. Unions, like any organization where leaders are periodically elected, are prone to playing politics. Working in an organization where a union is present is quite different from working in one where no union exists. Unions can be important assets to organizations, or they can be major liabilities. It is well known that some managers are so inept at practicing management that a union is essential to protect employees from being mistreated.

Union leaders can precipitate situations that cause complaints, just as they can work with supervisors and others to avoid them. Union leaders have been known to aggressively pursue worthless complaints, even through arbitration. They can also work to settle complaints informally and avoid the time and cost of formal discussions.

It is not uncommon for union stewards or committeemen to lack training for their leadership roles. Poorly trained or untrained leaders are prone to insecurity, prompting them to do things that eventually cause problems for employees, management, and themselves. Training for union leaders is just as important as it is for management. In most cases, management's behavior at all levels sets the climate for union and employee behavior. Good labor-management relations mean fewer problems in the long run. It is good business to manage in ways that create reasonably harmonious labor-management relations.

It must be understood that in a unionized organization, more formal complaints are somewhat inevitable. The reason is that the union leadership must justify its existence to the membership. Failure to do so invites charges of misrepresentations.

An employee's job, and conditions in the job environment, are sources of complaints. Any one or combination of the following can serve as underlying causes of complaints:

Being overtrained or undertrained for the job
Too much overtime
Rotating shift work
Excessive danger on the job
Unhealthy work environment
Conflict among employees
Low pay
Fear of change
Lack of understanding of personnel policies
Lack of understanding of the labor-management agreement

In trying to find out why an employee is complaining, it must be remembered that often the stated reason for the complaint is not necessarily the real reason. The employee himself may not even be aware of what is bothering him. The supervisor, who is usually the first person in management to be involved in hearing an employee's complaint, must attempt to find the underlying cause(s) in order to try to bring about a permanent solution.

As in the case of discipline problems, complaints can stem from causes outside of the organization, and even within the employee himself. As discussed, health, finances, or family problems affect employees on and off the job. Life on the job cannot be separated from life off the job.

The Importance of a Procedure for Handling
Employee Complaints

As has been discussed in various chapters, conflict between
people in organizations is inevitable. Employees, motivated to
serve self-interests, will view conditions and events differently
than managers. Conflict inevitably generates friction, and friction generates heat. Unless the heat is released, it will build to
explosive levels.

It is requisite that all organizations have some formal process for the systematic and timely review of employee complaints. A complaint-handling procedure is the best safety
valve any organization can have to release organizational heat
generated by conflict. An organization that does not have a
formal procedure risks creating perceptions of unfairness and
injustice. From feelings of unfairness or injustice, a sense of
grievance evolves. A sense of grievance among people is the
incentive that motivates them to retaliate. As discussed in
other chapters, retaliation can take many forms.

An employee complaint-handling procedure not only serves
to resolve problems, it can be used to prevent problems. When
employees are able to meet with supervisors and other members of management in a neutral environment, for example a
lunch room or conference room, mutual discussions can freely
take place. As those readers who have participated in complaint discussion meetings know, complaints are not the only
things that are discussed. Employee input on the effects of
possible, or pending, changes in the organization can be obtained. Employees' suggestions can be used to improve upon
ideas and plans. This helps to build cooperation and teamwork.

To an ever increasing degree, government is taking action to
safeguard employees' rights. Government intervention,
lengthy court proceedings, hearings, and investigations are
costly and time consuming. Often, the only people to benefit
are the attorneys, government agencies, and the courts,
whether the complaints are justified or not. This can happen
even if a complaint-handling procedure exists in the organization. Does this mean that a formal procedure for discussing

employees' complaints is unnecessary, because employees can go to outsiders anyway? The answer is no.

First, if an employee's complaint can be resolved internally, it is in the best interests of all concerned. Second, if the employee's complaint cannot be resolved internally, management has already gathered and reviewed appropriate information. Management is better able to defend its position. Outsiders are inclined to be prejudiced if they see evidence that management has not made an effort to determine if the employee's complaint has merit. Third, an employee's complaint does not exist in a vacuum. Other employees know what is going on. It is very difficult to keep things confidential or secret in any organization. If other employees feel that management has made a sincere effort to resolve the aggrieved employee's complaint, they may be less inclined to develop negative feelings about management. This occurs only if those employees who influence the thinking of most others perceive that, in general, management is fair. When influential employees perceive that management is generally unfair, any action taken by management can be distorted to mean the opposite of what was intended.

Essentials of Effective Complaint-handling Procedures

Any procedure for resolving employee complaints must function in an orderly and timely manner. Its objective must be to attempt to resolve complaints in a way that in the long run facilitates working relationships. The most meaningful measure of any system is employees' perceptions of its overall fairness.

Procedures for handling employee complaints vary widely. They range from highly structured to very informal. Either extreme is bad. A highly structured procedure can be too rigid; an unstructured procedure is open to misunderstanding and misinterpretation by all involved. It is not unusual to find that employees are unaware as to how a procedure works when it is very informal. All they may know is that if they have a problem, they may see their supervisor or take a complaint up to the president. This says nothing about investigations, responses, time limits, appeals, or whether complaints should be in writing.

All formal labor-management agreements, when a union represents employees, have structured grievance (complaint) procedures. Nonunion organizations are increasingly adopting structured programs. Some are remarkably similar to those in unionized organizations. The most important difference in nearly all nonunion organizations' procedures, compared to union-negotiated procedures, is a lack of provision for arbitration as the final step. Usually, management, instead of an arbitrator, has the final internal word. No procedure, whether a union represents employees or not, precludes employees from filing equal employment opportunity action, fair employment practices action, and civil charges against organizations and individual managers.

Whether the complaint-handling procedure involves a union or not, the role of the supervisor is essentially the same. Supervisors have a principal responsibility to manage in ways that do not cause chronic or excessive complaints. When complaints do arise, every reasonable effort must be made to settle the majority of complaints at the level where the complaint originated. On occasion, for reasons like the following, complaints must be referred to higher levels of the organization for possible resolution.

Supervisor lacks authority.
Supervisor is uncertain of authority.
Union or employee is playing politics.
Supervisor believes employee is wrong.
Supervisor believes employee is correct but higher management thinks the employee is wrong.
Policy is being questioned.
Timing is inappropriate to settle complaints.
Personnel policy is unclear or unstated.
Fear of setting a precedent for future cases.
Uncertainty about past practice in similar cases.

Complaint-handling procedures usually have a number of steps or levels. The normal range is from three to five steps. Four steps appear to be the most common. Whether or not an employee represents himself, is represented by another employee, or is represented by a union-appointed or -elected representative, all procedures should share certain common elements.

Before any complaint is put into writing, it should be discussed informally with the employee. The majority of complaints are usually settled in this manner, thereby eliminating the need for further formal processing. At this stage, responses to complaints can be oral.

If the employee is not satisfied, he should be required to state his complaint and what he wants in writing. The formal complaint should go to the aggrieved employee's immediate supervisor with copies to appropriate members of staff and management. In some organizations, the formal complaint is filed with a personnel or industrial relations department, with copies to other members of management.

The organization should have a stipulated time limit in which to respond to the employee or union in writing. Failure by management to adhere to a stipulated time limit at any level of discussion should be grounds for granting the employee's request. Time limit extensions should be available for unusual or extenuating circumstances; for example, a manager was ill or on vacation.

The complaint should be discussed between the supervisor and the employee, or a representative of the employee, to determine if it can be resolved. Management's formal answer to the complaint must be stated in writing. Specific reasons for approving or denying an employee's complaint and request should be given.

The employee or his representative should have a specified number of scheduled work days to either accept management's answer or appeal the complaint to the next level of management. At each level of discussion, the facts, circumstances, and conditions pertaining to the employee's complaint should be reviewed. Maximum limits for reviewing the complaint at each level of management must be stipulated. Management's formal written answer must also be given within specified time limits.

At each successively higher level of discussion, the participants in the discussions may change. Members of management almost always change. In a nonunion organization, the employee may participate at all levels of discussion because he is often representing himself. In a unionized organization, various members of the union's management hierarchy participate at different levels of discussion. The number of levels in a complaint-handling procedure usually depends on the structure of the organization. Too many levels or steps in a procedure cause time delays. Time delays are potential sources of problems. On occasion, time can work in favor of a situation, especially if it can be used to temper emotions. However, more often than not, time delays cause problems.

If the complaint is not dropped by the employee, or settled by management to the satisfaction of the employee, it may reach the final level or step of the procedure. In a nonunion organization, the final step is either the director of personnel, or similarly titled person, or the organization's president. In a unionized organization, the final step is arbitration. Whatever final action is taken by management, it should be communicated to the supervisor of the unit where the complaint originated. The reasons for the decision should also be explained. Failure to communicate this important information to supervisors has caused considerable problems in many organizations. Supervisors, in the absence of feedback, will develop their own reasons as to why higher-level management did what they did.

The Role of the Supervisor in Handling Complaints

Because the majority of complaints from employees arise due to some action supervisors did or did not take, supervisors' proper handling of complaints is very important. Supervisors must be trained in ways to avoid complaints as well as how to handle them when they arise.

In a unionized organization, supervisors must be trained in

interacting with stewards. To employees, a union is like an insurance policy. The steward is the employees' insurance agent and legal counselor. As such, he attempts to properly represent the interests of employees to justify that employees are getting their money's worth for the union dues they pay. Supervisors must also thoroughly understand the labor-management agreement and all changes in the interpretation of the agreement resulting from memorandums of understandings or grievance settlements. It is not unusual for union stewards to have more knowledge about the contents of the agreement and changes in interpretations of it than supervisors. Supervisors must take the time to read the agreement mainly because they have to abide by the provisions in it. Instead of reading the agreement and any changes that have occurred since its negotiation, supervisors often learn by the trial and error method. They make decisions, and if they are not contested by an employee's complaint, it must be okay. If an action or decision is contested and the supervisor loses, then he knows that he erred. This is a costly way to learn. However, this approach to learning is widely used by supervisors.

A union steward can be an asset, or a liability to a supervisor. The role of steward is very political because it is usually elective. Supervisors must be sensitive to the steward's political standing in a complaint situation. If stewards are politically secure, they can take more risk in trying to settle employees' complaints. If they are politically insecure, they will be prone to gamesmanship in order to survive in the role. This makes them unpredictable and often difficult to work with. Supervisors, by the way they grant or deny employees' complaints, can politically make or break stewards. The reverse can also be true. Stewards can make life miserable for supervisors by generating unnecessary grievances, pursuing worthless ones, or by entrapping and harassing supervisors.

Supervisors must recognize when it is better to grant a grievance they would rather not grant in order to strengthen a steward's position. Likewise, stewards must recognize when it is better to support the supervisor on an issue rather than an employee. The understanding of each other's role and where the give and take must take place is very important. A politically secure steward who basically is supportive of a supervisor can help the supervisor manage employees.

In the majority of nonunion organizations, employees represent themselves in pursuing complaints through the various steps. In a nonunion organization, the supervisor's role appears to be far less complex. However, because of an employee's apprehension, inarticulateness, and lack of comprehensive knowledge of personnel policies and practices, the supervisor often has a more difficult role. It is easy to take advantage of the employee. If the supervisor does this, it will eventually lead to perceptions of unfairness. Because of the problem of employees representing themselves, some nonunion organizations have developed complaint-handling procedures that allow employees to elect one of their peers to represent them. The employee usually has the option of pursuing the complaint alone or turning it over to an elected peer.

Whether or not a union is present, supervisors must be fully knowledgeable as to how the organization's established complaint-handling procedure works. They must abide by its provisions. They must also insure that employees understand their rights to use the procedure free from any reprisal actions whatsoever. If employees are too intimidated to file complaints, the procedure is worthless. Some complaint-handling procedures function like one-way doors. Filing a complaint is often a ticket to an eventual discharge.

When an employee, or group of employees, initiates a complaint, the supervisor should listen carefully to the complaint and the reasons for it. If the employee is emotional, he should be put at ease. Give him a chance to get the complaint off his chest. Some employees, because they have not developed the ability to plan and organize their thoughts and words, are prone to using emotions and profanity to express themselves.

While the employee is voicing his complaint, try to figure out if what he is saying is what he really means. As discussed, stated reasons for complaints are often not the real reasons. An employee may complain that his workplace is dirty, or that he is being overworked, when his real complaint may be that no one pays any attention to him.

An effective supervisor has learned to control his emotions.

This does not mean that he never displays emotions such as impatience or anger. He has learned to control the timing and intensity of his emotional releases. Getting into an argument with a complaining employee at the wrong moment can be disastrous.

A complaining employee intentionally, or unintentionally, may not tell the whole story, or have the facts straight. It is important that supervisors try to get the right facts and circumstances pertaining to the employee's complaint. It is important to learn to differentiate between facts and opinion. Before any action can be taken regarding the employee's complaint, it is usually necessary to investigate the situation. As in situations involving disciplinary action, a fair and impartial investigation of facts and circumstances pertaining to the complaint is essential.

The employees' point of view must be considered. Even if they are wrong, their reasons for believing they are right must be identified and carefully considered. Employees' motives in complaining must be assessed. Are these employees motivated by a sincere belief that they are correct, or are they playing a game? Supervisors must be cautious in prejudging employees' motives as well as the validity of their complaints. Snap judgments imply prejudgments.

Before any decision can be made, the situational climate must be considered. The long-run effects of any actions or decisions must also be considered. How other situations have been handled must be investigated and evaluated, and the danger in setting precedents for future cases must be considered. In important or possible precedent-setting situations, it is wise to consult with higher levels of management and staff professionals before making any decisions.

In responding to an employee's complaint, whether orally or in writing, words must be chosen carefully. Choosing the wrong words will cause misinterpretations and misunderstandings. It is important that the employee understand exactly what the decision is regarding the complaint and on what bases the decision is being made.

If the employee is dissatisfied with the decision regarding his complaint, he must understand his rights of appeal. He must understand the procedure to be followed in filing an appeal. Time limits must be made as clear as possible.

Any decision made by a supervisor should be communicated to higher management and staff professionals. It is also important to communicate the reasons for the decision and the reaction of the employee to the decision.

Questions Most Often Asked by Supervisors in Handling Employees' Complaints

Why do I have to listen to an employee's complaint? Can't I send him to the personnel director?

While the personnel director is trained in how to handle an employee's complaint, he is not the employee's supervisor, nor does he have to work with him on a day-to-day basis. The most important part of any supervisor's job is to develop a climate of trust, respect, and cooperation, so high production can be maintained. The supervisor is often in the best position to understand the employee as a person. By listening to an employee and attempting to resolve his complaint, a supervisor is strengthening his relationship with all employees. The supervisor and the employee live in a give-and-take environment and both must feel that they profit by the relationship. If a supervisor does not have the authority, or cannot handle the complaint because of its nature, then someone like a personnel director should be involved.

Some employees gripe and complain about almost anything and everything. Do I have to listen and respond to each and every complaint?

Not necessarily. An effective supervisor understands his employees. An employee who gripes about everything has problems that are deeper than what he is complaining about. The best approach is to try to identify the underlying causes for an employee's griping and then deal with them. In some cases, ignoring an employee can be useful. However, if used frequently, it is very dangerous. Ignoring complaints is akin to slapping the employee in the face. It is wise to try to work it out with the employee.

Do I have to give a reason to an employee when I either grant or deny his complaint?

Yes. Most employees are reasonably mature adults. Also, immature employees believe they are adults. Not giving reasons is like treating the employee as you would a young child. It will breed resentment and anger. Even if the employee may not like, or agree with your answer, it is better to tell him your reasons than it is to say nothing. In the absence of information, the employee will make up his own reasons and act upon them. That could cause problems for everyone.

Can I compromise with an employee on what he is requesting in his complaint, or is it an all or nothing situation?

There is no simple yes or no answer to this question. A number of factors must be considered. One's authority, organization policy, past practices, and the possibility of setting precedents must be considered. If a suitable compromise can be worked out, it may be best for all concerned. However, in some instances, a compromise would be out of the question.

To what extent should my boss participate in handling an employee's complaint?

This depends upon the roles defined in the complaint-handling procedure and the organization's practices. If you are required to confer with others before taking any action on a complaint, then you must do so. It is preferable that you try to handle the complaint yourself. However, under any of the following circumstances, you should discuss the complaint with others:

Uncertainty of authority.
Uncertainty about how similar situations have been handled in the past.
Complaint is of a highly sensitive nature.
Employee is highly emotional and could react violently.

In a union situation, can an employee withdraw his complaint at any time?

When a union is involved, for all practical purposes an employee cannot withdraw his complaint once the union is involved in representing him. At successive levels or stages of discussion, the employee who issued the complaint usually does not participate in the discussions. Unlike an attorney, the union steward cannot be terminated from his job as a steward on a moment's notice. Once the union is involved, it has assumed a degree of ownership of the complaint.

Am I bound by settlements to similar complaints when handling an employee's complaint?

Settlements of similar complaints should be used as guidance in settling a particular complaint. If the facts, circumstances, and conditions pertaining to and surrounding this complaint are similar to those in other complaints, then past practice should be followed. If the complaint at hand is somewhat different from others, then you are not bound by past practice. Wording of the response to the employee's complaint is very important. Care must be taken to avoid setting precedents, if that is not desirable.

In a union situation, does the union steward have to be present whenever an employee is discussing a complaint with me?

Unless specifically stated in the labor-management agreement's language, the answer is no. In most agreements, the employee has the right to request the presence of the steward. If you have a good relationship with the steward, the steward may be able to help you resolve the complaint. Therefore, you might ask him to participate. If the steward is troublesome, his presence should not be requested. If the employee insists on the presence of his steward, you have no choice but to include the steward.

Always having the steward present in discussing complaints with employees can be a dangerous practice. The steward's prestige and influence often increase at the expense of the supervisor. The strongest relationship must be between the supervisor and the employee, not the supervisor and the steward.

My organization has no formal system or procedure for handling employees' complaints. How should I handle complaints?

Just because a formal system or procedure does not exist is no reason to ignore complaints. To maintain an effective working relationship, you should let employees know that if they have complaints, they should discuss them with you. In handling an employee's complaint, follow all of the appropriate guidelines. Be willing to take the employee's complaint to a higher level if you believe that he is right. If you disagree with him, tell him the reasons for your disagreeing.

What is the most important thing to do in handling an employee's complaint?

Try to be fair and always be honest. To be fair, it is necessary to see the employee's point of view. To be honest, you must be prepared to act upon what you find out about the situation even if what you find is embarrassing. Once you lose your credibility with an employee, your relationship with him is severely damaged.

Why can a person like a personnel director override my authority? After all, he isn't my boss and he is not responsible for production.

The reason why someone like a personnel director, who isn't your direct boss, can override your authority is that he has authority on personnel matters. He must insure that your decisions are correct in light of prevailing organization policies and practices. He is responsible for the overall maintenance of good employer-employee relations.

I think that the employee's complaint is valid, but my boss and the personnel director do not agree with me. What should I tell the employee?

Tell the employee that you discussed the matter with higher-level personnel and the decision was not to acknowledge the complaint. Caution must be exercised in the degree to which you side with the employee. Understand higher management's position and communicate it to the employee even though you disagree with it.

What are the risks in trying to talk an employee out of his complaint?

The only risk is if you try to outwit the employee. Although the employee may be trying to outwit you, you should avoid getting down to his level. If you want to outwit the employee, think of the potential risks before doing it.

Those in higher levels of management never give me any feedback as to why they granted or denied an employee's complaint. I get my information from the grapevine. What should I do?

Make a sincere effort to educate those above you as to the reasons why you must be informed. Help them understand the problems that a lack of feedback causes. If that does not work, consider a transfer, or look for another job.

If I do not treat all employees' complaints the same way, I may have a discrimination charge filed against me.

If you treat all employees the same, you may also get a discrimination charge filed against you. When facts, circumstances, records, and conditions differ, your handling of complaints must differ. Be prepared to support your position with facts. Gut reactions, feelings, and the like will not be acceptable.

9

Establishing standards
and assessing
employee performance

ESTABLISHING performance standards or expectations and assessing actual performance against standards or expectations is an important part of the supervisory role. Employees need to understand what is expected of them in all aspects of their work. They must also understand that performance assessment is a continuous process, and the distribution of rewards is a function of actual performance.

The Need for Performance Standards

As has been discussed throughout the book, employees are motivated to seek rewards that are meaningful to them. They will plan, organize, direct, and adjust their behavior in ways to obtain such rewards. Their behavior is not necessarily logical, or even rational. Behavior is subject to perceptual distortion, incomplete information, inaccurate information, and emotions.

People want to believe that the ways they behave are right. They have a tremendous capacity to rationalize that their behavior is correct given particular facts, circumstances, and conditions.

In the absence of feedback as to whether their behavior is right or wrong, proficient or inefficient employees, from their perspectives, will conclude that what they have been doing is right and that they have been doing it well. They will expect to be rewarded by the organization for their behavior. If they are suddenly told that how they have been behaving is wrong, what they have accomplished is unacceptable, and that rewards will not be forthcoming, problems will occur.

Most employees do not continually try to improve their job performance. High achievers, according to a number of behavioral researchers, comprise only 5 to 10 percent of the population. They are the types of employees who continually set increasingly challenging goals and higher standards of performance for themselves. The large majority of employees who are not high achievers are influenced by a variety of factors which affect their aspirations, goals, needs, and job performance. Peer pressure is one significant factor. Unless supervisors establish and communicate performance standards, employees will be influenced by others to establish their own performance standards. It is not unusual to find that employees' standards for performance, or what they believe is a good job, are lower than the organization's standards or expectations.

Whatever standards or expectations for performance are developed, they must be communicated to employees. Employees must accept these standards or expectations as requirements of their jobs. Performance must be assessed, feedback given, corrective action taken when necessary, and rewards given to employees whose performance meets or exceeds standards or expectations. All of this is more easily stated than properly carried out.

Some organizations have comprehensive performance standards, well-defined appraisal or assessment programs, and trained managers at all levels to insure that performance is properly assessed and rewards are given for merit. Most organizations do not, and this causes considerable problems for supervisors and employees alike. When people think of standards their first thought is basic motion studies, commonly referred to as stopwatch standards, which often generate all kinds of negative feelings in employees and supervisors. Industrial or methods engineers tend to have bad images and arouse insecurity and other emotions whenever they start to time-study jobs. The author speaks from experience, since he worked as an industrial engineer, and later supervised industrial engineers. The tensions caused by attempting to time jobs, and the games played by management and employees to bias standards, often make the effort to establish standards not worth the time or cost. For these reasons, the use of time-study standards has declined. The use of time-study standards has also declined because of the complexity of jobs in interrelated work environments. In many organizations, jobs are so highly integrated that separating one job from another to establish standards is almost impossible. Does this mean that performance standards should not or cannot be established? The answer is no.

Many supervisors, higher-level managers, staff personnel, and employees have argued that standards for jobs cannot be established. Their arguments grow louder as work becomes less repetitive or routine. They argue that because many job activities vary widely on a day-to-day basis, it is impossible to obtain or develop meaningful measurements. These arguments lack merit because they are based on an assumption that a precise standard needs to be developed. There is virtually no job where some type of standard or expectation cannot be developed. Standards do not have to be precise. What is important is that employees have a clear understanding of what is expected of them. All employees develop their own ideas as to what constitutes good or bad performance. All supervisors do the same. The objective is for supervisors and employees to develop similar ideas about good or bad performance. To reach a common understanding, one of the following approaches must be used.

The organization, through higher management or staff, develops and imposes standards on supervisors and employees.

Supervisors develop standards and impose them on employees.

Employees develop their own standards and impose them on supervisors.

All parties negotiate in a give-and-take climate to reach a common understanding of standards.

Types of Standards

There are many types of standards in any organization. They can range from standards for personal hygiene to standards of product quality. The less analysis that goes into developing a standard, the higher the probablility that the standard will be inaccurate.

Many types of standards for behavior or job performance are based on history and tradition within a group or the entire organization. In fact, some organizations communicate their standards for service, product quality, and the like in their motto or logo. For example, "The Erie Is Above All in Service" is the motto and logo of The Erie Insurance Group, a successful regional insurance company. For some time, the Ford Motor Company used the symbol of a lightbulb and the words "Ford Has a Better Idea" to communicate its standards for innovation. Standards such as these often become a tradition. Employees at all levels are expected to live up to the organization's standards.

Historical standards, while usually of high value in influencing employees' behavior, can have an opposite effect. Some organizations and supervisors do not change standards or adjust to changing needs and conditions. Traditions and past practices verbally expressed as "we have always done it this way," or "it was good enough for me, therefore, it's good enough for you," and the like, can impede rather than enhance performance. Historical standards, whether they are organization-wide or unique to a particular group, must be continually assessed against changing needs. When necessary, they must be changed.

Another class of standards are the engineered standards. These types of standards are usually very precise. They are developed through careful analysis and measurement. They may be developed through records analyses, as in the case of cost standards. They can also be developed by use of time studies, or time and motion studies in the case of defining normal output in a given period of time for the average worker. Some jobs more than others lend themselves to precise measurements. Many machine and man-machine operations in factories and offices can benefit by using engineered standards if they are properly developed and applied.

Standards may also be expressed as objectives or goals. An objective, whether it is to reduce absenteeism, improve quality, increase profits, or whatever, is a standard of performance that is trying to be achieved. Setting objectives and goals gives individuals or groups of employees something upon which to focus their efforts. The process known as Management by Objectives (MBO) involves the establishing of standards of performance or accomplishment that employees are required as part of their jobs to attempt to achieve. Contrary to popular opinion, managing by objectives, per se, is nothing new. People, as individuals and in groups, have been planning, organizing, and directing their behavior to reach objectives for tens of thousands of years.

A class of standards that often cause problems are the subjective standards: feelings, attitudes, or vague or general statements. All organizations have many varieties of subjective standards that may vary widely within any one organization. What constitutes good or bad performance in one group can be quite different for another. Standards of dress, etiquette, adaptiveness, cooperation, integrity, courtesy, morality, just to name a few, tend to be more subjective than objective. There is nothing wrong with subjective standards, per se. Many types of behavior and activities cannot be precisely or sometimes even generally prescribed. The main problem with subjective standards is developing a common understanding of what each standard means. The greater the degree of difference in interpreting what the standard is, the greater the degree of variance in behavior from the standard. This, of course, often leads to the necessity for disciplinary action.

Traditionally, standards have been viewed as part of control processes. Standards do serve to establish limits for behavior and performance, which does make them control mechanisms. However, standards should also be used for development purposes. By establishing standards that employees have to strive to reach and maintain, supervisors help employees to develop as workers and human beings. Accomplishment and achievement usually serve to generate feelings of pride, satisfaction, respect, and dignity.

Once standards or expectations are established, they must be communicated. Employees' performance, as compared to standards or expectations, must be assessed to determine which employees meet or exceed standards and which employees do not meet minimum standards. Rewards to reinforce desired behavior, and discipline to influence a change in unacceptable behavior, must correlate with standards or expectations.

The Performance Assessment Process

Performance assessment usually means the formal process or act of measuring how well an employee has handled assigned duties and responsibilities during a given period of time. Performance assessments are used for a variety of purposes. They are used in compensation administration, promotional consideration, disciplinary consideration, transfer, layoff, assessing training needs, and other procedures. One of the most important benefits to be gained from performance assessment is the strengthening of relationships between supervisors and employees.

The person who has the primary responsibility for assessing employees' performance is the supervisor. Most supervisors have little, if any, training in how to properly assess employees' performance. As noted earlier, this causes no end of problems. Performance assessment is not a once a year process, where a supervisor dusts off some antiquated form given to him by the personnel department and goes through the process of checking boxes and writing a few comments in an attempt to inform an employee how well he has or has not performed. It is a continuous part of the day-to-day working relationship between a supervisor and employees.

Most supervisors do not get highly enthused about having to formally assess employees' performance. In fact, many would rather not do it at all. They give all types of reasons: "It is not important"; "I know my people"; "I do not have the time." These excuses and many other defense mechanisms show that some supervisors are at best apprehensive, and at worst terrified of having a face-to-face discussion with employees about their performance. They are, essentially, afraid of getting into a situation where they cannot cope with the possible consequences. The author has even known of cases where an employee's performance assessment is sent to his home. He does not see it until he opens his mail. If he does not like what he reads, he has no opportunity to discuss his feelings. Sounds incredible; nonetheless, it is true.

Most employees want feedback on how they are performing in relation to standards or expectations. They also expect to be rewarded for their contributions to the organization. All organizations must develop performance assessment systems that can consistently and, if properly used, accurately measure employees' performance. It goes without saying that rewards must be geared to performance. It is the responsibility of higher management to thoroughly train supervisors in conducting assessments, and to insure that the learning is correctly applied. Supervisors must understand that their own performance assessments are in part based on how well they can assess the performance of their employees.

This section will not cover in depth the design of performance assessment or compensation systems. Responsibility for the design of valid and reliable systems rests with staff specialists. Proper system design is important. It is virtually impossible to get good results with a poorly designed system, unless supervisors ignore the system or learn to work around it. That happens more frequently than most people realize. Over the years, many supervisors have told the author how they have learned to work around a poorly designed system. To avoid game playing with assessments, supervisors must believe that the system they are using is properly designed. Their input into a system's development can be valuable to all concerned. A properly designed system will not work unless supervisors are given thorough training, guidance, counseling, and coaching. It often takes years before a supervisor can exhibit high proficiency in assessing employees' performance.

Even without a formally developed system, supervisors can still assess employees' performance. Performance assessment as a process has been around for thousands of years. A properly designed system facilitates the process and minimizes problems. The keys to successfully using performance assessment with employees are: (1) employees understand what is expected of them, (2) they are informally assessed continually, (3) they are appropriately rewarded or disciplined, and (4) they have a right to discuss their feelings and concerns.

Assessing an employee's performance is often referred to as letting him know where he stands. Informing an employee as to where he stands, or an employee's asking where he stands, is subject to varying interpretations. It is similar to asking a person how he feels. How a person feels is a relative thing. In relation to a sick person, he may feel fine. However, in relation to someone who is very healthy, he may feel terrible. Letting an employee know where he stands normally refers to one employee's position in relation to other employees, or his position in relation to a standard which he is being compared to or against.

However, where an employee stands can also affect any of the following:

When do I get a raise?
How much of a raise will I get?
I deserve a promotion!
Am I going to be fired?
Does anyone know that I am alive?
Does anyone care that I am alive?

Am I accepted around here?
Does anyone appreciate my efforts?

Not all employees favor formal assessments. Poor or marginal employees, especially, dislike them. Employees whose job performance is based on subjective rather than objective standards recognize that judgments based on impressions or gut feelings can vary widely. Last, employees who receive built-in feedback automatically on performance tend to see little useful purpose in a formal review.

Before any performance assessment program can be developed and implemented, employees must understand the responsibilities and duties of their jobs, the purposes of performance assessment, the bases on which their performance will be assessed, and the types and limits of the rewards and discipline to be given in conjunction with performance or lack thereof. They must also know their rights of appeal for perceived unfairness and the channels and procedure to be followed in appeal.

An employee's formal performance assessment is influenced, even sometimes predetermined, by events and conditions that occur long before the formal face-to-face meeting. Relationships and interaction between supervisors and employees are important. If supervisors and employees cannot express their feelings and opinions without reasonable candor, then the formal performance assessment meeting will be approached with reluctance, suspicion, and even fear. The fewer surprises that occur for supervisors and employees in an assessment meeting, the more effective the assessment will be for all. It is the supervisor's responsibility to establish and maintain a climate where accurate, timely, and open communication can exist.

Supervisors and employees who have poor working relationships will find the assessment experience painful. In this type of climate, more problems will be created or inflated than will be discussed and resolved. Under these considerations, it may be better not to have supervisors conduct formal assessments. This does not mean employee relationship problems will go away; eventually they will worsen. In this type of environment, time and money would be better spent correcting basic relationship problems rather than concentrating on assessments. Once the climate improves, a formal assessment program can be implemented to strengthen relationships.

Performance assessment is composed of two parts, observation and evaluation, and both are subject to bias. Whatever type of system or approach is used, the possibility of bias and prejudice affecting judgments exists. Bias and prejudice problems may be caused by poor system design, interpersonal relationship conflict, differing expectations, and various situational and organizational factors.

Identifying and Overcoming Problems in Employee Performance Assessment

A valid and reliable system with comprehensive training for all levels of management in the conducting of performance assessments is essential. Barriers or factors affecting performance assessments must be recognized and either overcome or controlled.

Lack of knowledge about what an employee is responsible for, or what an employee has or has not accomplished during a given period of time, is a common problem. This is why position descriptions and performance standards or expectations are essential. However, unless supervisors interact frequently with employees to monitor performance, problems will occur. This doesn't mean that a supervisor must go to every one of his employees daily and find out how many beans they have counted that day. Trying to be that precise is more akin to harassment than managing. However, some types of jobs do require daily monitoring, or bean counting.

Good employees require less monitoring of performance than poor employees. Good employees should not be ignored because they are doing their jobs well. Their behavior needs to be reinforced by the supervisor occasionally letting them know they are doing well. Poor employees need to understand that they must change their behavior or suffer the consequences for poor performance.

Supervisors, like all other people, have their biases and

prejudices. Effective supervisors learn to control their personal feelings and remain objective. Prime examples of prejudice in performance assessments are age, job tenure or seniority, sex, religion, ethnic origin, and race. Supervisors, like everyone else, have a tendency to characterize and stereotype people. Such stereotyping as these are common.

Men are better suited or qualified to do this type of work. Therefore, it is obvious that a man will do a better job than a woman. Examples might include: operating heavy equipment, driving a forging hammer, cupola loading in a foundry, or stevedoring on a dock.

Women are better suited or qualified to do this type of work. Therefore, it is obvious that a woman will do a better job than a man. Examples might include: secretary, file clerk, switchboard operator, receptionist, airplane flight attendant.

Older employees have reached their full potential. Therefore, we should not waste time training and developing them for higher levels of work. Besides, they will be leaving us soon.

Young employees have more potential to develop than older employees. They should receive the training and development.

Young employees are immature. We can't give them high levels of authority and responsibility until they are older. They must have a few gray hairs to show they have matured.

Besides the possible violations of law for demonstrating these types of biases or prejudices, there are the practical contraindications to demonstrating these biases or prejudices. When employees recognize that obtaining rewards is based on things over which they have no control, problems will eventually surface. The best way to minimize these prejudices and biases is to demonstrate that they will not be tolerated.

Performance assessments are also affected by situational and organizational factors. An employee's popularity can affect his assessment. It is easier to assess an unpopular employee as a poor performer than to assess a popular employee the same way. An employee's relationships with others, especially higher-level managers, is a significant factor. The author remembers a case where a young woman who was a marginal performer was dating a vice president who happened to be the immediate supervisor of the woman's supervisor. The woman's supervisor was afraid to assess her performance accurately for fear of how his supervisor would react. The best way to deal with this type of problem is to demonstrate to supervisors that a person's popularity or unpopularity is not a criterion for performance assessments. Actions, of course, will always speak louder than words.

Employees' or supervisors' perceptions of how rewards are really given rather than how they are theoretically given is another factor. Employees at any level will rationalize all types of behavior to obtain rewards. If apple polishing or boot licking is the name of the game, then this will be the behavior many will exhibit. Those who refuse to play the game, or do not know how to play the game, will tend to become jealous and resentful. This can be a real problem if the better employees become resentful because rewards are given on bases other than performance. The most effective way to deal with this problem is to make certain that performance is the name of the game, and it is the only game in the organization.

How closely employees work with their supervisors and how frequently they interact with them can influence a performance assessment. The saying "out of sight, out of mind" is appropriate. Employees who work closely with their supervisors are able to influence the supervisors' perceptions almost continually. If they create a bad impression one day, they can change it in a short period of time. Employees who do not see their supervisors often have no such advantage. The supervisors' impressions are formed by what others say, or when interaction does occur. Of course, the opposite effect could also exist. Employees who project a positive image and do not see their supervisors often have less of a chance of supervisors' perceptions changing than the employees who are seen by their supervisors daily.

The availability of rewards is another factor affecting assessments. When rewards are scarce, there is a tendency to spread them evenly across the board. The rationale is that since there is so little to go around, it does not pay to attempt to discriminate among employees. The same logic can also apply when rewards are plentiful. The rationale then is that, having done well, management can afford to be generous. In times of high inflation and limited money for raises, the tendency among supervisors and employees to want raises across the board can be very strong. The best way to handle this type of problem is to give raises and other rewards solely on the basis of merit, or to give a small percentage across the board and the remainder on merit. As an example, if a supervisor is allotted 5 percent of his budget for raises, he could give 5 percent across the board. This, of course, would create mediocrity. It would be better to discriminate among employees on the basis of merit. A high performer might receive 10 percent and a low performer might receive nothing. Depending on the salaries of the two employees, that could average 5 percent between them.

Employees learn to play upon their supervisors' personal sympathies to get larger raises and other rewards. Depending on a supervisor's personal sympathies, employees may avoid dressing in expensive clothing, complain about the high cost of living, drive an old car to work and remark on how it needs to be continually repaired because a new one is just too expensive, or pass remarks about how they cannot afford to pay for the children's education. They also might bring peanut butter and jelly sandwiches for lunch and say they wish they could afford to buy lunch out or purchase expensive luncheon meats. They might talk in the supervisor's hearing about how others are so well off because their spouses make a lot of money and their own spouse has to work just so their normal expenses can be paid. Some may mention the high expenses they are incurring for the care of an aging relative.

These tactics tend to increase when performance assessment time draws near. The best way to handle this type of politicking is to ignore it. The more a supervisor reacts positively to these types of games, the more they will be played. Eventually it will lead to one-upmanship among the employees. Employees who engage in this type of behavior will try to outdo their peers, and simultaneously try to discredit their peers' remarks.

Another class of organizational barriers are traditions and past practices. Traditions like rewards for length of employment in the organization are not uncommon. Another statement that is often heard is, "We take care of our senior employees." An employee's tenure of employment or seniority should not be heavily weighted for reward purposes. Traditions and past practices should be retained only if they facilitate or reinforce performance of employees.

Supervisors often permit their own values and perceptions to affect judgments about employee performance. Supervisors may have thoughts like these:

If I assess my employees' performance as below average, I will be saying that I am an ineffective supervisor.

I have only high-performing employees in my group. I discharged the poor performers a long time ago.

If I tell an employee that he is not doing well, it will have a negative effect on our relationship.

I am an effective supervisor, therefore my employees do their jobs well.

I am an ineffective supervisor, therefore my employees do not do their jobs well.

If I get high raises for my employees, it will increase my effectiveness with them. They will perceive me as a supervisor who can get rewards for them.

New employees in my group should not be assessed as being higher than average for the first couple of years. As time passes, I can assess them higher to show how they have developed under my supervision.

These types of biases can be reduced by training and having higher-level managers review performance assessments with supervisors before and after meetings are held with employees.

One of the most pervasive of all errors in assessing employees' performance is the so-called halo effect error. The halo effect occurs when an employee is judged on the basis of an overall impression that the supervisor gains from certain traits and characteristics that are observed or thought to have been observed in the employee. Based on this partial information, the supervisor develops an overall or gut feeling about the employee. Gut feelings can be accurate, but they are often prone to error because they are based on emotions, not facts.

Overall impressions of employees are more likely to occur when the assessment is based on (1) a characteristic or trait that is of moral importance to the supervisor or others; (2) only a few characteristics or traits from which overall conclusions are drawn; (3) the supervisor's inability to properly assess his observations; or (4) the influence of others upon a supervisor's judgments.

Closely related to the halo effect are the biases that occur when an assessment of one performance factor is allowed to spill over into another factor. For example, because an employee is assessed low on attendance, it is only logical that his quantity of work must be low. This may or may not be true. Supervisors, like anyone else who assesses someone else's performance, can be prone to rationalize or use logic to draw conclusions about an employee's behavior. This use of logic or rationalization is often faulty. For example, one might conclude that if an employee cannot get along with others, he cannot possibly do a good job. Again, this may be true, but it is not necessarily the case. An employee whose performance is totally dependent upon his own efforts could be a high performer and not get along with others. On the other hand, if an employee's performance is dependent upon the cooperation of others and he cannot get along with people, his performance would probably suffer accordingly.

Another type of error that is most often observed when examining the assessments of a group of employees is the statistically normal distribution error. The performance of the members of any group is usually not evenly distributed. Some will perform better than others. Some type of a distribution or statistical curve exists. Figure 11(a) shows a normal or typical bell-shaped distribution. In this example, the majority of the employees are acceptable. The curve can be shifted to the right or left of center. If it is assumed that the majority of employees in the group are superior, then the distribution of performance assessments for the group would shift to the right as shown in Figure 11(b).

The distribution of a group of employees' performance assessments is irrelevant if it can be supported by facts about individual and group performance. If supervisors can consist-

Figure 11. (a) Assessment category, normal. (b) Assessment category, superior.

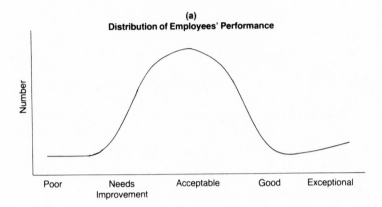

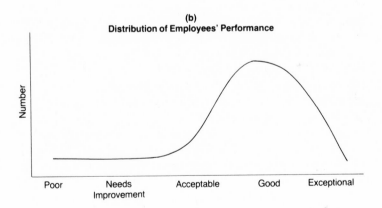

ently and accurately measure individual and group performance, then the individual and group assessments will corre-
spond with actual performance.

Guidelines for Supervisors in Conducting Performance Assessments

Supervisors must view performance assessment as a primary
responsibility and a way to facilitate cooperation and maintain
the performance of all employees at a high level. Performance
assessments must also be viewed as an employee-development
and counseling tool. High performance must be supported and
reinforced by the appropriate financial and nonfinancial rewards. Behavior and performance that do not meet standards
or expectations must be handled through discipline and the
withholding of rewards. Performance assessments must be
used as a tool to assist employees in developing their potential
so that they can achieve many of the things they aspire to in
their positions and careers.

Supervisors who do not recognize the necessity and importance of employee performance assessment, or who are not
sufficiently trained in conducting assessments, will find that
discussing performance with an employee is very stressful.
The following guidelines can be employed in reducing the
stress associated with a face-to-face discussion of performance
with an employee.

A performance assessment is not something a supervisor
does at the last moment and then hands to the employee. It is
an activity that must be carefully planned. In preparing for a
performance assessment meeting, it is important to use all
available records so that opinions can be supported by facts.

The employee's performance for the entire time period, for
example, six months or a year, must be considered. It is important not to overemphasize unusual or isolated incidents that
are not typical or characteristic of the employee's normal performance. A supervisor should not be influenced by previous
assessments. A change in the level of performance does not
necessarily mean that the present or previous assessment is

incorrect. It does suggest, however, that an inquiry be made into the reasons for the change in performance.

Most performance assessment systems identify a number of performance factors. For example, quantity of work, quality of work, cooperation, adaptability, interpersonal relations, work habits, job knowledge, and attendance. It is important that halo and spillover effect errors be avoided. Each factor should be considered as distinctly as possible from all other factors. Be careful not to compare one employee with another. Employees' performance should be compared against standards or expectations, not against one another.

It is important not to allow an employee's level or length of service affect the performance assessment. An employee with a lot of skill and experience should generally be held to higher standards of performance than an inexperienced employee. Because an employee has been doing a particular job for many years does not necessarily mean that he is a high performer. Nor is it necessarily true that an inexperienced employee will perform at a lower level than an experienced employee.

A performance assessment meeting should not be rushed. As a guideline, three-quarters of an hour to an hour should be budgeted for a meeting. Keep the meeting private and keep telephone or other interruptions to an absolute minimum. A supervisor should not allow himself to be influenced by compensation considerations: the employee's need for money, high inflation, or the few dollars that have been budgeted for raises should not be considered in the assessment. Even if there were no money available for raises, performance assessments should be conducted.

A supervisor should not be afraid to go on record with his opinion about an employee's performance. Performance assessment meetings do not always run smoothly. This is especially true when an employee is being told that his performance is below standards. Some employees are very skillful manipulators and will use emotions, fears, prejudices, intimidation, hostility, and even threats to influence the outcome of their assessment. A supervisor who has prepared himself for an assessment meeting will have anticipated an employee's behavior and will be able to handle situations that may arise.

During a performance assessment meeting, the most important thing a supervisor can do is listen and learn. The employee should be given the opportunity to talk about his own perceptions of his performance. If a disagreement exists, the supervisor should ask himself, "Can I support my opinions about this employee's performance?" The meeting must be viewed as having a constructive rather than destructive purpose. If an employee's performance is not up to standards or expectations in any or all areas, it is the supervisor's responsibility to help the employee to see that his behavior needs to be changed. If an employee's performance meets or exceeds standards or expectations, his behavior needs to be reinforced by rewards.

In closing a performance assessment meeting, the supervisor should accomplish the following:

- Summarize what was discussed during the meeting.
- Restate what has been mutually agreed upon during the meeting. Areas of disagreement and the reasons for them should also be restated.
- When the need for improvement has been discussed, it is important to have a clear understanding of the employee's specific intentions, or lack thereof, to change behavior.
- The employee should be informed of the rewards that will be recommended. If his performance has been unacceptable, he should clearly understand the possible consequence if he fails to change his behavior.
- It may be advisable to suggest or schedule follow-up meetings.

After the meeting has ended, the supervisor should review in his own mind what was accomplished during the meeting.

10

Employee counseling

WHEN counseling is mentioned, the thought that might come to people's minds is that of a person being treated by a psychiatrist or psychologist. Psychoanalysis is an effective way of helping people overcome emotional problems. Psychoanalysis, which is based on Freudian theory, holds that mental illness, especially neuroses and character disorders, results from unconscious conflict in a person's mind. Most behavior problems do not require the use of psychoanalysis. Psychoanalysis is something that requires considerable skill and training to use effectively, and should never be attempted by supervisors because they lack the training or time to properly do it.

For the purposes of this book, counseling will be broadly defined. Employee counseling is a communicative relationship between two or more people whereby one person or group uses various techniques and approaches to help a person help himself to resolve an existing problem, avoid a potential problem, or make a decision.

Counseling is an implicit part of every supervisor's relationship with his employees. All supervisors should receive some minimum training in how to identify potential or existing behavior problems in employees. Supervisors should also have training in basic techniques and approaches in helping employees help themselves to resolve, overcome, or avoid problems. Last, supervisors should be able to recognize when an employee's behavior problem is serious enough to be referred to professional counselors for treatment.

As has been discussed throughout this book, effective supervisors learn to develop positive working relationships with their employees. This can be accomplished only when a climate of mutual trust, respect, and confidence exists. Supervisors who do not have the training, or the desire to help employees who are experiencing behavior problems, will not be able to build positive working relationships. Counseling employees should not be limited to problem solving or avoidance; it should also be used as a feedback and development tool. Such a tool provides a channel for supervisor-employee communications and focuses on who is performing and what their desires, expectations, and aspirations might be.

From time to time, each of us comes face to face with personal problems. Problems may be work related, stem from conditions outside of work, or stem from conflicts within ourselves. Most people, with minimum difficulty, are able to resolve their problems without any assistance from others. However, as life becomes complex with resultant stresses and strains, it appears that to a greater degree today than in the past, people are having difficulty coping with or resolving problems. Statistics on crime, delinquency, divorce, the use of drugs, and the rise of cults support this view. Some people recognize when they need the help of others and take necessary steps to obtain it. Most people either do not recognize the need to seek help or are reluctant to seek it.

Supervisors, whether they like it or not, are often thrust into counseling roles. This is particularly true when the supervisor is someone whom employees respect and trust. An employee may turn to his supervisor, or to a close friend, or, in unionized organizations, to the shop steward. Sometimes this is at the expense of the supervisor's prestige and influence. When an employee's behavior problems affect his job performance or relationships with others, the supervisor has no other choice but to become involved.

Because supervisors are leaders, employees will look to them for guidance. To some employees, their supervisor is a father figure. Supervisors who are trusted and respected will find themselves being asked for their advice and opinions on matters that touch all parts of an employee's life. An untrained supervisor may experience anxiety, apprehension, depression, and even suspicion and fear when he is unable or unwilling to counsel an employee who has asked for assistance.

Benefits and Risks of Supervisors Counseling Employees

Perhaps the most important benefit of becoming involved in employee counseling is that it gives supervisors the opportunity to get to know employees better. Supervisors who understand how their employees think, feel, act, and react are better able to build productive working relationships. Supervisors who take the time to help employees overcome problems, or make decisions, will find that their prestige and influence with employees will increase.

Counseling is beneficial to employees because it gives them the opportunity to reduce anxieties by getting things off their chest. Most problems employees have to cope with can be resolved or controlled if the employee is able to sort things out for himself and then make a decision on a course of action. Talking things out is an effective way of putting a problem in its proper perspective and laying the groundwork for developing a solution. Because an emotionally troubled employee's ego will activate defense mechanisms to protect itself from psychological injury, it is difficult for the employee to face the reality of the problem. If employees are unwilling or unable to face the reality of the problem, development of a solution becomes remote. Counseling can be effectively used to stimulate problem-solving behavior. Through counseling, emotionally troubled employees can be influenced to accept the reality of the situation. From there, various approaches to coping with or resolving a problem can be identified and assessed.

Emotionally ill employees are usually dependent upon others to help keep them out of difficulties, or get them out of difficulties they cannot get out of by themselves. As long as employees remain dependent upon others, their problems will persist. An important principle of counseling is that employees must learn to help themselves; if counseling is successful, it helps employees develop a sense of responsibility.

While the benefits to employees are significant, counseling is not without its risks and dangers; it is somewhat like opening a box the contents of which are unknown. What may appear to be a minor problem affecting an employee's behavior may turn out to be the tip of deep-seated emotional illness or character disorders requiring the type of assistance that supervisors are not equipped to give. A supervisor who tries to treat an employee who has severe psychological or social problems will usually end by doing more harm than good for the employee and himself. Counseling takes time; a supervisor who supervises 20 or more people may find that he cannot afford to take away from production time to counsel employees. This can be especially true in a highly production-oriented work environment.

For these two reasons, that is, the risk and time involved, supervisors should never attempt to treat an employee who has a serious emotional problem or character disorder. What a supervisor must be able to do is recognize the possible seriousness of a problem and see to it that the troubled employee is referred to professionals inside or outside of the organization for treatment. Referral should be made to others even if it is only suspected that a problem is potentially serious. In the handling of possibly severe emotional problems or character disorders, it is better to be safe than sorry. Referral should first be made to higher-level managers or staff professionals before a recommendation to seek professional help outside of the organization.

Another risk in counseling employees is the nature of the supervisor-employee relationship. It is virtually impossible for any supervisor to counsel an employee with complete, detached professionalism. The supervisor shares in the employee's problem if it is having an effect on job performance. Even under the best of conditions, it is difficult for employees to be totally open with supervisors. Supervisors are authority figures and their decisions affect the welfare of employees. Employees will always experience some anxiety, apprehension, suspicion, and even fear when discussing problems with their supervisors. This is especially true when sensitive or confidential matters are discussed. There is always a question or concern about how information is going to be interpreted and acted upon.

A supervisor's knowing highly sensitive or confidential information about an employee could consciously, or unconsciously, let it affect his feelings or judgments about the employee. It would be difficult for adverse information about an employee's health, marital relations, or moral character not to affect feelings or judgments about the employee. For example, even though epilepsy is usually controllable with medication, a social and psychological stigma is often attached to a person who has this condition. A supervisor may consciously or unconsciously find reasons to reject a qualified employee who has epilepsy for a promotion to a position of higher responsibility.

Another problem associated with supervisors counseling employees is the personal relationships that may exist. Familiarity can and occasionally does affect objectivity. On the other hand, an employee's perception of the ability of a supervisor to act as a counselor may be negatively or positively affected by familiarity. To some employees, their supervisor is a person who is all knowing and all seeing. To other employees, their supervisor is just another person who possesses and exhibits all of the faults and weaknesses associated with human nature.

Recognizing Emotional Illness in Employees

In general, any significant change in an employee's behavior occurring within a relatively short period of time is cause for concern. When people are contronted with problems and pressures that are seemingly insurmountable, strong feelings of anxiety or guilt may evolve. That part of the human mind called the ego cannot operate properly under strong feelings of anxiety, guilt, or other pressures. To protect itself against these pressures, the ego activates defense mechanisms. This activation process can be either conscious or unconscious. In effect, when people are confronted with pressures which they cannot properly handle, they call upon their defense mechanisms to protect themselves from psychological injury.

Emotional illness in employees is characterized by their consciously or unconsciously using defense mechanisms. What differentiates so-called normal from emotionally ill people is the degree to which defense mechanisms are used. With the exception of sublimation, all emotional illnesses or character disorders are characterized by the abnormal use of one or more of the following defense mechanisms.

Repression. Repression is the underlying basis of all defense mechanisms. Through repression, people keep threatening desires, wishes, fantasies, feelings, and memories in their unconscious. If repressed feelings and thoughts move to the conscious part of the mind, the ego exerts energy to push it back into the unconscious. For example, if something very derogatory is said about someone a person greatly admires, that person may pretend not to hear what was said. All supervisors have been exposed to situations where employees selectively hear what they want to hear, or see what they want to see. Pretending not to hear or see something that was actually heard or observed is evidence of repression.

Rationalization. Rationalization is the process by which a person imagines or substitutes acceptable reasons for doing something that are altogether different from the real reasons. For example, an employee may rationalize that his reason for working so hard is to be a better provider for his family, when the real reason is that he works for self-fulfillment. Phrases like "I am doing this for my family," or "I am doing this for my company," or "I am doing this for your benefit and not my own" are commonly heard.

Sublimation. Sublimation is the process where an unacceptable behavior is channeled into an acceptable behavior. The drive or desire to say or do something that would be socially unacceptable is channeled into a socially acceptable outlet. As an example, a person with a strong desire to commit acts of violence may become a football player. By the use of sublimation, people can be very creative and effective while releasing a potentially destructive drive.

Projection. Projection is the mechanism by which a person's ego transfers to someone else something it cannot accept. For example, a person may not trust himself and may be unable to accept this; in order to avoid the tension and anxiety of having to handle this knowledge, the person will project it onto others by saying that no one can be trusted.

Displacement. Displacement is the process by which a part may come to symbolize the whole or vice versa. As an example, a person who had a bad relationship with an obese supervisor may exhibit negative feelings about all supervisors who happen to be obese.

Identification. Identification is the process by which an unacceptable feeling or belief may be made acceptable by identifying it in someone else who personifies it. For example, a person who has a strong prejudice against blacks will not openly express his prejudice, but will identify strongly with someone who openly professes the same prejudice.

Regression. Regression is the process by which people withdraw from a situation they cannot cope with to a situation they can manage. For example, a person may regress into childish behavior which, from his perspective, makes him better able to deal with situations and events. In extreme form people can withdraw in a fantasy world and be completely detached from reality.

Self-punishment. In conflict and stress situations, it is not unusual for people to want to inflict some degree of pain and suffering on someone else. If a person cannot bring himself to inflict some injury on the intended recipient, he inflicts the injury upon himself.

Reaction formation. Reaction formation is the defense mechanism whereby an undesirable feeling or impulse is kept in the unconscious by strong emphasis on its opposite. For example, a person may intensely dislike his supervisor, but be very friendly toward him.

Substitution. Substitution is the process whereby something that is desired or highly valued, which cannot be possessed for psychological reasons, is unconsciously replaced by something that can be possessed and is psychologically acceptable.

Fantasy. Fantasy is the defense mechanism in which a person constructs something in his mind that he cannot have or experience in reality. For example, a person may have a desire to be an army general. Since he cannot achieve his goal, he fantasizes that he is one.

Conversion. Conversion is the process in which a person converts a psychological conflict into a physical symptom. For example, a person may be afraid of having to do a newly assigned job and subsequently develops a physical problem to avoid doing it. Also, an employee may develop a headache or stomachache when his problem is that he is worried about failing an upcoming job proficiency test.

Compensation. This is the process whereby a person who has a physical impairment or psychological deficiency emphasizes some other activity or behavior that serves to compensate for the limitation. For example, a person confined to a wheelchair may compensate for his physical limitation by intellectual achievement.

Denial. Denial is the defense mechanism in which the ego refuses to accept, or severely distorts, something that is obvious. As an example, a person who has been denied a promotion may continue to believe that his promotion notice is delayed because of a paperwork backlog or has been lost in the mail.

As people increasingly use any one or combination of the aforementioned defense mechanisms to protect their egos, their behavior will become increasingly abnormal. Abnormal behavior or emotional illness in a mild form is known as neurosis. Abnormal behavior or emotional illness in extreme forms is known as psychosis. Neurotic behavior is often observed in the form of anxiety (which embodies feelings like tension, uneasiness, distress, and frustration), phobias, obsessions, compulsions, mild depression, extreme fatigue, and hypochondria. Psychosis, referred to as character disorder, is observed in the form of schizophrenia, paranoia, obsessive-compulsiveness, manic-depressive brhavior, masochism, and extreme antisocial behavior. Character disorders appear to be in part inherited and in part due to environmental factors. Character disorders that are caused in part or totally by chemical imbalances or genetic abnormalities cannot be successfully treated by counseling. Neuroses and environmentally caused psychoses can be treated by counseling.

Considering the complexity of human behavior, and the obvious limitations in supervisors' ability to counsel employees, employee counseling must be approached with caution. As noted earlier in this chapter, supervisors, whether they want to or not, must be involved in counseling employees with problems. Techniques and approaches to counseling can vary widely. They can range from informal employee gripe sessions to psychoanalysis conducted by a clinical psychoanalyst. Supervisors, for obvious reasons, should use only the most basic approaches to counseling.

The Nondirective Approach to Counseling

The nondirective or client-centered approach to counseling is different from advice giving and other diagnostic approaches because the counselor does not direct the employee's behavior or even give him advice as to how he should behave. The focus of this approach is for the person being counseled to discover his problems himself and work out a solution that fits his value system and therefore is acceptable to him. The nondirective approach is a good one for supervisors to use because it avoids the need for making a diagnosis and also avoids the problems associated with making an incorrect diagnosis.

Supervisors engaging in nondirective counseling should make it clear that they have a genuine interest in the employee's welfare and development. They must recognize the importance of counseling as part of their job responsibilities, but accept their limitations and not attempt to be psychoanalysts. As counselors, supervisors must accept or tolerate employees' different values and attitudes and try not to pass judgments on those values. Supervisors should also help employees to accept responsibility for their own behavior and to realize that they are capable of helping themselves to cope with or resolve their problems in ways that conform to their own values, beliefs, feelings, and attitudes.

Nondirective counseling requires supervisors to develop effective listening skills, which for many supervisors is not easily achieved. This can be especially true for supervisors who have strong personalities and who are outgoing and assertive. Listening is more than refraining from speaking. Effective listeners avoid showing anger, surprise, joy, sympathy, agreement, or disagreement with whatever employees say. Supervisors should be as nonjudgmental as possible, because the basic objective of nondirective counseling is to help employees help themselves. Avoiding making judgments does not mean that supervisors cannot inform an emotionally ill employee who asks for certain information; information should be given, unless the employee is seeking the kind of thing that will reinforce his own view.

In nondirective counseling, the proper technique of interviewing is essential to achieve the best possible results. In the nondirective approach, the employee must feel at ease. The time and place of the meeting are important, and should be convenient for the supervisor and the employee. The setting for the counseling meeting should permit the employee to be psychologically at ease. If the meeting is held in the supervisor's office, he should avoid sitting behind his desk. The desk establishes an unequal and judgmental climate and inhibits communication. A conference room or even the lunch room, if there is privacy, would be more appropriate than an area where the employee is psychologically uncomfortable.

It goes without saying that confidences should be maintained. Because a supervisor is an authority figure, it is difficult even under the best of conditions for employees to express their true feelings. Considerable discretion should be used in handling sensitive or confidential information. Sometimes a problem or the solution to a problem may involve other employees. When this is the case, the supervisor should discuss possible courses of action with the employee being counseled before taking any action. This should be done to avoid any possibility that confidences have been betrayed if actions are taken without the employee's knowledge.

In the counseling meeting, the supervisor should attempt to get the employee to speak openly. The room setting and the time of the meeting help, but the essential ingredient is the communication skill of the supervisor. Phrases or questions like "I see, would you like to tell me about it?" "I think I understand," and "Would you help me to better understand your feelings?" are nonjudgmental and can be used effectively to bring the employee's feelings into the open.

It is not unusual for employees to stop talking during a counseling meeting because they are unsure of what they want to say next or are looking for an indication of agreement or disagreement. While a supervisor may feel great pressure to break the silence by saying something, it is better to let the employee initiate further conversation. A supervisor should initiate a conversation only if there is a danger of the meeting collapsing because of the stress and tension that can build during a period of silence.

Experienced supervisors have long recognized that what employees complain about often is not what is really bothering them. The same analogy can be applied to counseling. Employees may talk about a wide variety of things that are causing them concern or frustration. Sometimes the employee's remarks will even be contradictory. It may take some time before the things that are the cause of the employee's problems can be identified and discussed.

As part of the nondirective technique, the supervisor should learn how to reflect upon what has been said by the employee. Some people believe that the nondirective approach to counseling means that the supervisor is passive throughout the meeting. This is incorrect. Any discussion between two people, if it is to be productive, requires a give-and-take environment. While the employee should do most of the talking, the supervisor must contribute to the discussion. Instead of contributing by giving advice, which would be contrary to the nondirective approach, the method of reflecting upon what the employee has said should be used. In order to reflect successfully upon what an employee has been saying, the supervisor should develop an understanding of what the employee means rather than what he is saying.

The method of reflecting feelings requires that the supervisor serve as a reflective mirror, restating each of the key things that are said by the employee. Key feelings must be reflected so they can be reviewed, discussed, and analyzed. In reflecting upon key feelings, the details and nonessential information are allowed to fall by the wayside. For example, employees may present all kinds of reasons for believing that they have been treated unfairly. The supervisor would reflect upon the employee's statements by restating the key point, that is, the belief that the employee has been treated unfairly. In reflecting, it is important to avoid using the employee's exact words, phrasing a question, or drawing a conclusion. If the employee believes that he has been unfairly denied a raise, the supervisor should state, "You feel that you have been treated unfairly." This is a statement of what the supervisor believes is the employee's feeling, not a question or a judgment.

Another important consideration in reflecting an employee's feelings is to be certain that the feeling that is actually expressed is reflected. If the supervisor attempts to diagnose or anticipate the employee's feelings, the counseling relationship may be damaged.

It is not unusual in a counseling meeting for an employee to communicate mixed feelings or make contradictory statements. The supervisor should not attempt to point out the obvious inconsistencies to the employee, but should attempt to understand the bases for the inconsistencies. Asking the employee to restate what has been said may help to clarify feelings and understandings.

If an employee becomes emotional during a counseling meeting, the supervisor should let him work through his emotions and become directly involved only if the employee gets very depressed, hysterical, or enraged. After an emotional release, it is not unusual for an employee to feel shame or guilt. If the employee wants to discuss his emotional release, he should be allowed to talk freely about it.

When an employee displays feelings of confusion, hostility,

insecurity, fear, rejection, and the like, the supervisor could reflect upon possible solutions or courses of action brought out by the employee during the conversation. Caution must be exercised in avoiding pushing the employee toward a course of action he may not be ready to accept for himself. Remember, the objective of nondirective counseling is for the employee to develop a solution to the problem and not for it to be developed and imposed by the supervisor.

Giving Advice as an Approach to Counseling

As an approach to counseling, giving advice can be useful. Many problems that employees face are relatively simple, and giving advice can save time and energy and enhance relationships. Obviously, giving advice as a form of counseling should not be considered when it is suspected that the employee has an emotional illness or character disorder. In giving advice, it is important for the employee to know that it comes from the supervisor's perspective and experience, and that the advice may or may not fit the employee's situation and values. The employee must understand that he, and he alone, must make the final decision on whether to accept or reject advice. If this precaution is not taken, it is easy for the employee to misinterpret the supervisor's intentions or words. Many a supervisor has given advice with the best of intentions only to have it backfire on him. Advice should be given only after it is felt that the employee is genuinely seeking it and is able to properly assess how to act or react. The more serious and personal the employee's problem, the more cautiously advice should be given.

Supervisors who are asked for advice should preface their advice by statements like "From my experience," "The way I view the situation," or "If I were in your situation, I would consider." The use of such prefatory remarks helps the employee understand that the advice is being given from the supervisor's perspective.

In giving advice, supervisors must be careful to avoid diagnosing an employee's problem and recommending a solution that, from the supervisor's perspective, will resolve the problem. The risk is that the wrong problem may be identified, and the solution may not fit the employee's value system. In addition, the employee may be unable to carry out the recommended course of action. Finally, the recommended course of action may turn out to be entirely wrong and produce disastrous results. In summary, supervisors can, and should, give advice to employees when it is sincerely requested. However, it must always be given with caution.

Counseling and Its Relationship to Employee Job Status

Supervisors, higher-level managers, and staff professionals recognize that employees will experience legitimate physical, psychological, or social problems at some point in their lives. It is also well accepted that employees are valuable assets and as such are long-term investments. Every supervisor who becomes involved in counseling an employee who has serious problems comes face to face with the question: "To what extent should the employee's situation affect his job status?" There are no set formulas or easy answers to this question. A lot depends upon past and prevailing practices, the quality and length of the employee's service, past performance, potential, and the extent to which the problem persists or may reoccur.

When a decision must be made regarding the job status of an employee with serious legitimate physical or mental problems, the supervisor should seek the advice and counsel of higher-level managers and staff professionals. As a guideline, if the problem is seriously affecting his job performance or relationships with others, the employee, in addition to receiving counseling, should be considered for a medical leave. A leave should be considered if the employee's record warrants that he has earned one, and it is believed that a leave will help the employee overcome or control his problem(s). Although the employee's employment is secure for the duration of the leave, raises and promotion may not be forthcoming, because he is not performing on the job and therefore has not earned a raise or promotion. If the problem(s) cannot be overcome, and depending upon the facts and circumstances pertaining to the case, the employee should be placed on permanent disability, transferred to a position where he can make a contribution, be subject to disciplinary action up to and including suspension with the intent to discharge, or be retired.

While organizations must be sensitive and compassionate toward employees' problems, no business organization is a social welfare agency. Employers and employees alike pay taxes to support government social agencies and social programs. Business organizations have an overriding obligation and responsibility to survive and prosper in order to serve society's needs effectively and efficiently. To this end, employees must understand that no matter how real their problems are, there is some point at which the organization can no longer retain them if they are consistently unable to meet minimum job requirements.

11

Time management

TIME is a unique and valuable resource. It is something that all people have, although the specific amount available to any one person is unknown. When people are young, they tend to view the amount of time available to them as inexhaustible. When people are old, they recognize that their supply of time is running out. Time is precious because the amount available to any one person is relatively fixed. Few people live beyond 100 years. For the majority of people, life ends in the seventies.

Most people, supervisors included, waste time almost continually. The waste or mismanagement of time is a primary underlying cause of many management problems both on and off the job. Until relatively recently, few books, training programs, or seminars dealt with the subject of time management.

If a person were to make a comparative study of the lives of successful and unsuccessful people, one difference would be that successful people get more accomplished in less time than other people; they use their time more efficiently. Time management is the application of management to the use of time. Effective managers of time have learned how to make time count rather than counting time—how to effectively plan, organize, use, and control their own time and the time of others. In effect, time management is activity management.

Time management is important not only on the job but in every aspect of living. The first step in learning how to better manage time is to analyze how it is used. Supervisors, as leaders, must also study how to manage the time of others and how others with whom they have to interact manage their time. In a world where people are to varying degrees dependent upon one another, how others manage their time can greatly affect how we manage ours. Whether waiting for a slow clerk at a checkout counter or for someone to complete a task before one can start, others' wasting time does affect our use of it.

When analyzing something in an attempt to judge whether it is good or bad, reference points or standards are necessary. Without standards or reference points, it is impossible to make meaningful comparisons. When analyzing the use of time, it is important to ask these questions:

Am I doing it in a way that I think is the best?
Am I using the time to get what I think are the best results?
Should I change?
If yes, how should I change?
Should someone else do it?
Should it be done at all?
Should it be done at another time, or in another place?

To facilitate analysis of the use of time, it is suggested that a log of daily activities, noting time spent doing them, be maintained. A time and activity log is essential because it can be reviewed and evaluated in relation to objectives, standards, and priorities. It is important to identify the activities and events that caused the waste of time.

Common Time Wasters

Following are twenty common time wasters. This list is not all inclusive by any means: '

1. Scheduling too much time for a task. Work can and often does expand to fill the time available.

2. Being overwhelmed by the amount of work and conflicting demands. This causes stress which in turn causes the person to develop defense mechanisms which can lead to a further waste of time.

3. People have a tendency to procrastinate doing things that they do not like or want to do.

4. Fear of losing control, or fear that it will not be done right if someone else does it are two of the biggest reasons underlying supervisors' failure to delegate. Trying to do everything yourself often wastes time because you have no time to manage.

5. Lack of plans, objectives, goals, and priorities on a daily, weekly, monthly, and longer periods. People without a sense of direction or purpose waste time.

6. Poorly defined or ambiguous plans, goals, objectives, priorities.

7. Poor organization of thoughts and activities. Poor organization often displays itself as sloppiness. Having things in their proper place and having a proper place for things is important. Well-organized people know where things are located and do not have to waste time looking for them. A well-organized person projects an image of efficiency.

8. Fear of loss of status, prestige, and even one's job are significant causes of wasting time. Some people create unnecessary work and activities in order to look busy. They fear that if they do not look busy by coming in to work early, working into the lunch hour, or taking work home they will lose prestige. All organizations have employees who play these games.

9. Inability to say no. Some people just cannot bring themselves to say no. This happens whether they are dealing with a spouse, children, friends, salespersons, bosses, peers, or employees.

10. Poor habits are another major time waster. Human beings, to a degree, are creatures of habit. Many of people's daily activities are built around patterns and habits. As goals and priorities change, habits should also change.

11. Too many interruptions. Most people allow themselves to be too easily interrupted. Throughout any and every day,

someone or a group will try to use our time for their benefit. Unless people understand their needs, goals, and priorities, they will be prone to unnecessary interruptions. In general, the more important or influential a person is, the more people will try to infringe upon their time.

12. The telephone is a very useful instrument for communicating. It is also a major source of interruption and time wasting.

13. Many supervisors who have offices keep their door open all the time. This is in keeping with the so-called open door policy. Keeping the door open is an invitation for someone to enter. There are times when the door should be closed and even locked.

14. Time is often wasted by too much socializing. Socializing is an important aspect of people's lives. However, a person's inability to terminate a discussion, telephone call, or a meeting usually leads to a waste of time.

15. Receiving and reading unnecessary mail. Some people have to be on every mailing list both on or off the job. To some, receiving a lot of mail or being on information distribution lists is a source of prestige and status. Taking the time to read mail that is unimportant wastes time.

16. Meetings on the job are a fact of life. While some meetings are essential, many are unnecessary. What is even worse is the time wasted in important meetings because of political gamesmanship by participants.

17. As has been shown consistently by various tests and observations, most people are poor readers. A poor reader wastes time because he reads slowly and is slow to comprehend what he has read.

18. Failure to measure and assess how time has been spent is another time waster. Unless people have feedback as to how effectively time has been used, it is difficult to know whether present behavior should be continued or changed.

19. Indecision is another time waster. Some people never have enough information on which to make a decision and consequently end up not making any decisions. Others fear being wrong and attempt to avoid mistakes by not making decisions. Both waste time.

20. Wasting time attending to details that could be handled by others or should be disregarded.

Considering the aforementioned time wasters and others not mentioned, supervisors should determine the extent to which they misuse time by reviewing their own daily activities. The best way to solve or overcome any problem is to first identify the underlying causes. The remainder of this chapter has been devoted to offering suggestions and approaches that supervisors can use to resolve or overcome common time management problems.

Planning

The first step in better managing time is to become time conscious. Time-conscious supervisors are continually sensitive as to how well their time, as well as the time of others, is used. Supervisors themselves should develop a daily plan of activities, recognizing the fact that not everything always goes according to plan. Depending upon the type of work activities that are supervised, supervisors should also require their employees to develop and use daily plans. A daily plan does not have to be an elaborate minute-by-minute schedule; it can be as simple as a list of what needs to be done that day. Once planned activities are listed, they should be compared against goals and priorities. This analysis often results in changes in planned activities. The final plan should serve as a guide for the day's activities.

The next step in using a daily plan is to organize the day's activities in some type of logical sequence and estimate the amount of time that should be budgeted for each activity. The organization of activities into logical groups always results in increasing efficiency. For example, most people spend their Saturdays making numerous trips to the supermarket, drugstore, bank, gas station, hardware store, discount store, and other places. Making a list of what needs to be purchased at each store and arranging the trips in a logical sequence results not only in saving time but also money. Time is saved because duplication is eliminated. Money is saved by reducing the use of the automobile and by purchasing only what is on a list. Studies have shown that shoppers who stick to carefully developed shopping lists spend less money than those who shop without lists and buy on impulse.

As the day progresses, the planned activities need to be compared against what is being accomplished. New activities may be added and others deleted. At the end of each day, the planned activities should again be compared to what was actually accomplished. The reasons why certain activities were not accomplished should be analyzed. This type of feedback increases awareness about the use of time and facilitates planning and organization. Whatever was not accomplished on one day should become a priority item for the next day. Improvement goals should also be established.

Supervisors who plan their activities to meet objectives and stick as close as possible to the daily plan will accomplish more in less time. They will also accomplish it better than if they did not have a plan. The more accurate supervisors are about their needs, goals, and priorities, the more they can accurately plan and schedule their activities. The more accurate the plan, the less they will be compelled to deviate from it.

Organization

Supervisors who plan ahead also learn to become better organized. Planning and organization go hand in hand. A word of caution about organization is in order. Some people are so highly and fastidiously organized that they become compulsive. Overorganized people can become so highly structured that they are unable to adjust or adapt to changing conditions. Extremes of any type of behavior can be dangerous.

It is difficult to describe an optimum level of organization or planning; the important thing is to make better use of time. It is also important to remember that the best plan is worthless if it is not followed.

In a materialistic society such as that in the United States, people have a tendency to surround themselves with possessions that they do not really need. Reducing the number of possessions and putting them in prescribed places can help people be better organized. This applies both on and off the job.

Organization of information is important. Supervisors are required to maintain all types of records, and reference to records and other types of information occurs daily. Developing a classification system and maintaining records in a timely and orderly manner are effective ways to reduce time spent looking for information. A little time spent each day or week on keeping records up to date and discarding information that is no longer needed will pay high dividends. Whether on or off the job, be it cooking recipes, appliance and equipment maintenance or repair manuals, bills for purchases, or receipts, a record-keeping system, a place to keep records, and the timely maintaining of records will pay the same dividends as are paid for record-keeping efforts applied on the job.

Supervisors should become adept at using the wastepaper basket. What is not currently needed or will not be needed in the future should be thrown away. The wastepaper basket is very handy to have around when reading mail, memorandums, and other forms of written information.

Establishing and communicating priorities

Supervisors in particular are subject to many demands on their time. It is not unusual for some of the demands to be conflicting. Stress can facilitate achievement or it can destroy life. The key to successful stress management is to direct the stress into productive activity. Demands upon time should be prioritized. The priorities of time and activities should be communicated to others. This can help reduce conflicts in demands and help others understand why their demands cannot always be met when they expect them to be met. Agreement to the priorities by others may not always occur. However, communicating priorities is far better than having them develop their own conclusions.

Pocket cassette recorders

To facilitate the use of time, supervisors should learn how to use dictating equipment. Pocket dictators are relatively inexpensive and pay for themselves almost immediately. Use of dictating equipment, aside from saving time by not writing, pays an added dividend: dictation requires planning and organizing thoughts and words. Pocket dictators are also very useful in making a record of certain thoughts. Creativity does not always occur on the job; creative ideas can come at any time of the day, and they often come when they are least expected. Unless the idea is captured on tape or paper, it is apt to be lost. The pocket recorder solves the problem. Supervisors in factories are usually on their feet most of the day. As they tour the factory they observe things or others bring things to their attention. It is difficult to remember everything that is seen or heard. What often happens is that by the time the supervisor gets back to his office, he has forgotten some of what he saw or heard. Again, use of a pocket recorder can eliminate that problem.

Controlling interruptions and socializing

Interruptions are a fact of life and cannot be eliminated; however, they can be controlled. Staying busy is a good way to reduce interruptions as people are less inclined to interrupt someone who is busy. They will readily interrupt someone who is idle. As mentioned earlier, closing the office door and even locking it at certain times of the day can be very effective in reducing interruptions.

In any socializing situation, the time of two or more people is involved. The central time-management question is: Who is controlling whose time? On the job, supervisors should interact with employees. It is better to visit employees at their work areas rather than having them come to visit you, because it is easier for you to walk away from a conversation. When an employee, or anyone else is in your office, it is not so easy to walk away or terminate a conversation. This guideline does not always apply. For many reasons, especially if discipline is involved, you may want the employee to come to your office. Also, while more skill is required, it is possible to control socializing when an employee is in your office. The main thing to be remembered in socializing is the purpose of the visit. Once the objective is achieved, continued socializing is unnecessary.

When employees or others socialize with you, letting them know how much time you have available can be effective.

Caution must be exercised in telling others how much time of yours they can use. Rudeness, abruptness, or aggressiveness can impede communication. Tact and diplomacy should be the guiding principles. Letting others know that you have to attend a meeting, keep another appointment, make some telephone calls, complete some reports, or even go to the bathroom can be effective ways to terminate a social visit without being rude or abrupt.

Time spent socializing can also be reduced if a stand-up meeting is held. If a visitor sits in a comfortable chair, he can become glued to it. This can be especially true in cases where employees have to stand at their jobs or work in somewhat unpleasant conditions. Employees can easily stretch a work break by coming into the supervisor's office and spending time talking while sitting in a comfortable chair. The author has observed many instances in factories where employees would go to their supervisor's air-conditioned office and socialize just to get away from the heat and noise of the factory. Under these conditions, employees sitting in comfortable chairs in an air-conditioned office will always prolong conversations. Carrying on a discussion while standing almost always reduces the time spent conversing.

Managing telephone calls

Few supervisors have the luxury of a personal secretary who can screen visitors or telephone calls. Higher-level managers generally have secretaries, but do not always use them properly. The key to managing telephone conversations lies in how the conversation starts. Questions about the weather, sports, politics, or the caller's health will always lengthen the time spent on the telephone. Conversations should be kept to the purpose of the call. If callers want to talk about the weather, politics, or sports, advise them that you need to know specifically what they want or need to know in order for you to help them. The same techniques for controlling telephone conversations can be applied to calls placed or received off the job.

Managing mail

Junk mail is not only received at home. Most organizations generate too much paperwork; large organizations especially tend to bureaucratize themselves by generating paper. Ego, prestige, pride, status, power, and influence are all associated with the generation and movement of paper. The first way to avoid having to handle unnecessary information is to get off the mailing or distribution lists both on and off the job. The next approach is to learn to distinguish important and unimportant mail. Although it may be difficult to track down the source of the organization that is selling your name to anyone and everyone, it is easier to do so at home than on the job. It is important to learn how to screen mail. When it is addressed to occupant or has a mailing label affixed, it is usually less important than mail that is personally addressed. Looking at the return address to see who sent the mail facilitates screening.

Mail received at home or on the job can be screened by reading the first couple of paragraphs of a letter and quickly scanning the rest of it. If in the first few paragraphs the contents appear to be unimportant, it should be immediately discarded. If in doubt, read further and then decide whether the letter requires action.

Improving reading and writing skills

The nation's educational systems have failed to teach people how to read. As a result, many people are slow readers and do not readily comprehend what they have read. Supervisors who recognize this problem in themselves or others should take steps to correct it. Popularly advertised speedreading courses can be helpful, but they are not essential. Continuing education courses in high schools and colleges, and practicing reading, can help significantly.

Consonant with improving reading skills is the improvement of writing skills. Poor readers are often poor writers. Good writing requires planning and organization skills. Many good books and courses are available to help improve writing skills; the time and money spent will pay dividends many times over.

Indecision

Supervision requires making decisions. All decisions involve the use of time, and they also involve an element of risk taking. Supervisors, like all other leaders, normally do not enjoy or want to make mistakes. Fear of making mistakes, or worse, failing, can and does lead to indecisiveness. Caution or prudence in making decisions is one thing; indecision is quite another. Sometimes the line between caution and indecision is very thin. Successful leaders have learned that mistakes will occur in decision making. It can be said that it is better to make a decision and be wrong than not to make a decision at all. The key to avoiding indecisiveness is to gather information quickly, sort and evaluate it quickly, examine the alternatives, weigh the consequences, and then make the decision. Invariably, some decisions will turn out to be wrong. It doesn't pay to wallow in guilt or self-pity. The mistake should be used as a learning experience to guide future decisions.

Controlling meetings

Meetings are a fact of organizational life. Useful ways to reduce time spent in meetings are to attend only those that are necessary and to know when to schedule them. Effective supervisors use their skills to influence and, as necessary, control the behavior of others in meetings. It is important to remember that people are prone to use the forum of a meeting to pursue their personal objectives, which may be at others' expense. Following are some questions and suggestions that may prove helpful in planning, conducting, and participating in meetings.

- Is the meeting necessary? Can what needs to be accomplished be better accomplished another way?
- The agenda for the meeting should be carefully planned and communicated in advance to those who will participate. Hidden agendas or additional items for discussion should be kept to an absolute minimum.
- Restrict the number of people required to attend. As the number of participants rises arithmetically, conversation rises geometrically. Two separate small group meetings may be better than one large group meeting.
- Set a time limit; meetings, like work, can expand to fill the time available.
- Be sensitive to the arrangement of tables and chairs, seating certain people together or apart, acoustics, and comfort.

- The time that a meeting is scheduled is important. Meetings scheduled at 1:00 or 2:00 P.M. often last the entire day. A 4:30 or 5:00 P.M. meeting does not drag on. People want to get home. Meetings held before the start of the normal working day can also be very effective.
- An effective leader keeps the conversation at a meeting close to the agenda and knows how to corral the politicians and gamesmen.
- Meetings have a tendency to never start on time. Consequently, participants learn to show up late. Some people even make a game of showing up late for meetings. To them, it is an assertion of their power to make others wait for them. Start meetings on time and do not be afraid to remind late comers that you start your meetings on time and you expect them to be there on time.
- End meetings when they are scheduled to end.

Managing details

All jobs require some attention to details. Although higher-level managers can often assign details to others, supervisors usually have to tend to details themselves. Details of any job should be evaluated against objectives, priorities, and job requirements. Supervisors who find themselves overburdened with details should prepare and present a case to higher-level managers to request clerical, technical, or administrative assistance. Cost-benefit analysis of a supervisor's time and energy in relation to a nonsupervisory employee's time and energy is necessary for showing higher-level managers how and why time and money can be saved by using other employees for some detail work.

Delegating to others

Delegation of tasks to others is an effective way to use time, but it is not easily accomplished. Many factors must be evaluated in deciding how many activities or decisions should be delegated and to whom.

For a number of reasons, supervisors and higher-level managers often fail to delegate to the degree to which they could or should. Fear of losing control or loss of status and prestige are perhaps the strongest reasons for not delegating. It is not easy to develop trust and confidence in others to the point where they can be allowed to do things that, if not done properly, would adversely affect our welfare. It is also difficult to allow others to do things that we could do better ourselves. Following are some examples of the most common reasons supervisors fail to delegate, and why employees often do not want to have activities or decisions delegated to them.

There is no room for mistakes.
Irresponsibility or untrustworthiness of employees, supervisors, or both.
No confidence in employees.
Employees have no confidence in themselves.
Fear of loss of status and prestige.
Supervisors think no one is as competent to do the job as they.
Jealousy.
No time to explain.
Cannot spare any people.
Employees are too inexperienced.
Inability to explain things clearly.
Fear of making mistakes, or of others making mistakes.

It is every supervisor's responsibility, as part of the supervisory role, to help employees develop. It is part of every employee's development to learn to accept responsibility. Teamwork cannot possibly exist unless people are willing to accept responsibility. Supervisors who learn to delegate to others are in the long run more effective managers. Some people confuse delegation with abdication. A common response to being asked why more delegation does not take place is, "I will lose control over employees." If delegation is not carried out properly, abdication will result. Some control, or the right to exercise control, is always necessary to insure that cooperation and productivity continue. However, the more responsible employees are, the less control needs to be imposed upon them.

Supervisors who delegate to employees are imposing responsibilities upon them. They are also giving employees the right to exercise, or the opportunity to develop, authority. Supervisors must retain the right and ability to restrict employees' use of authority, or take it away from them altogether if it is misused. Herein lies the key to avoiding abdication. Supervisors who do not retain authority, or lose the ability to take it back, abdicate their power.

From a time-management perspective, supervisors who delegate to others increase the results that can be obtained. One person can accomplish only so much; a well-managed group sharing responsibility can accomplish much more. Supervisors who delegate to others also have more time to use for more important work. Employees who willingly assume responsibility usually gain confidence through achievement and, in effect, become better employees. Better employees cause fewer problems; therefore, supervisors spend less time having to exercise discipline and control.

Assessing Management Skills

Supervisors' effectiveness in using time is affected not only by how they manage themselves, it is also affected by how well they manage their employees. Supervisors who are untrained, lack confidence, are insecure, jealous, or petty will waste valuable time having to resolve problems they cause or create. Supervisors, as has already been adequately discussed, are leaders and as such must set the proper examples of behavior. They must, through the use of rewards and corrective action, influence employees to exhibit desired behavior and meet expectations and standards. The application of good management is in itself the best way to more effectively use personal time and to influence others to properly use their time.

Index